58th Annual Meeting of the Association for Computational Linguistics (ACL 2020)

Tutorial Abstracts

Online
5 – 10 July 2020

ISBN: 978-1-7138-1374-3

Printed from e-media with permission by:

Curran Associates, Inc.
57 Morehouse Lane
Red Hook, NY 12571

Some format issues inherent in the e-media version may also appear in this print version.

Printed with permission by Curran Associates, Inc. (2020)

For permission requests, please contact the Association for Computational Linguistics at the address below.

Association for Computational Linguistics
209 N. Eighth Street
Stroudsburg, Pennsylvania 18360

Phone: 1-570-476-8006
Fax: 1-570-476-0860

acl@aclweb.org

Additional copies of this publication are available from:

Curran Associates, Inc.
57 Morehouse Lane
Red Hook, NY 12571 USA
Phone: 845-758-0400
Fax: 845-758-2633
Email: curran@proceedings.com
Web: www.proceedings.com

ACL 2020

The 58th Annual Meeting of the Association for Computational Linguistics

Tutorial Abstracts

July 5, 2020

Introduction

Welcome to the Tutorials Session of ACL 2020.

The ACL tutorials session is organized to give conference attendees a comprehensive introduction by expert researchers to some topics of importance drawn from our rapidly growing and changing research field.

This year, as has been the tradition over the past few years, the call, submission, reviewing and selection of tutorials were coordinated jointly for multiple conferences: ACL, AACL-IJCNLP, COLING and EMNLP. We formed a review committee of 19 members, including the ACL tutorial chairs (Agata Savary and Yue Zhang), the EMNLP tutorial chairs (Banjamin van Durme and Aline Villavicencio), the COLING tutorial chairs (Daniel Beck and Lucia Specia), the AACL-IJCNMP tutorial chairs (Timothy Baldwin and Fei Xia) and 11 external reviewers (Emily Bender, Erik Cambria, Gaël Dias, Stefan Evert, Yang Liu, João Sedoc, Xu Sun, Yulia Tsvetkov, Taro Watanabe, Aaron Steven White and Meishan Zhang). A reviewing process was organised so that each proposal receives 3 reviews. The selection criteria included clarity, preparedness, novelty, timeliness, instructors' experience, likely audience, open access to the teaching materials, diversity (multilingualism, gender, age and geolocation) and the compatibility of preferred venues. A total of 43 tutorial submissions were received, of which 8 were selected for presentation at ACL.

We solicited two types of tutorials, including cutting-edge themes and introductory themes. The 8 tutorials for ACL include of 3 introductory tutorials and 5 cutting-edge tutorials. The introductory tutorials are dedicated to reviewing, ethics and commonsense reasoning in NLP. The cutting-edge discussions address interpretability of neural NLP, multi-modal information extraction and dialogue, stylized text generation, and open-domain question answering.

We would like to thank the tutorial authors for their contributions and flexibility while organising the conference virtually. We are also grateful to the 11 external reviewers for their generous help in the decision process. Finally, our thanks go to the conference organizers for effective collaboration, and in particular to the general chair Dan Jurafsky, the website chairs Sudha Rao and Yizhe Zhang, the publicity chair Emily Bender, the ACL anthology director Matt Post.

We hope you enjoy the tutorials.

ACL 2020 Tutorial Co-chairs
Agata Savary
Yue Zhang

General Chair

Dan Jurafsky, Stanford University

Program Chairs

Joyce Chai, University of Michigan
Natalie Schluter, IT University of Copenhagen, Denmark
Joel Tetreault, Dataminr, USA

Tutorial Chairs

Agata Savary, University of Tours, France
Yue Zhang, Westlake University, China

Table of Contents

Conference Program

Sunday, July 5, 2020

6:00–9:30 (10:00–13:30) *Interpretability and Analysis in Neural NLP*
Yonatan Belinkov, Sebastian Gehrmann and Ellie Pavlick

6:00–9:30 (10:00–13:30) *Integrating Ethics into the NLP Curriculum*
Emily M. Bender, Dirk Hovy and Alexandra Schofield

6:00–9:30 (15:00–18:30) *Achieving Common Ground in Multi-modal Dialogue*
Malihe Alikhani and Matthew Stone

10:00–13:30 *Reviewing Natural Language Processing Research*
Kevin Cohen, Karën Fort, Margot Mieskes and Aurélie Névéol

10:00–13:30 *Stylized Text Generation: Approaches and Applications*
Lili Mou and Olga Vechtomova

15:00–18:30 *Multi-modal Information Extraction from Text, Semi-structured, and Tabular Data on the Web*
Xin Luna Dong, Hannaneh Hajishirzi, Colin Lockard and Prashant Shiralkar

15:00–18:30 *Commonsense Reasoning for Natural Language Processing*
Maarten Sap, Vered Shwartz, Antoine Bosselut, Yejin Choi and Dan Roth

15:00–18:30 *Open-Domain Question Answering*
Danqi Chen and Wen-tau Yih

Tutorial Proposal: Interpretability and Analysis in Neural NLP

Yonatan Belinkov
Harvard University and MIT

Sebastian Gehrmann
Google AI

Ellie Pavlick
Brown University

Abstract

While deep learning has transformed the natural language processing (NLP) field and impacted the larger computational linguistics community, the rise of neural networks is stained by their opaque nature: It is challenging to interpret the inner workings of neural network models, and explicate their behavior. Therefore, in the last few years, an increasingly large body of work has been devoted to the analysis and interpretation of neural network models in NLP.

This body of work is so far lacking a common framework and methodology. Moreover, approaching the analysis of modern neural networks can be difficult for newcomers to the field. This tutorial aims to fill this gap and introduce the nascent field of interpretability and analysis of neural networks in NLP.

The tutorial will cover the main lines of analysis work, such as structural analyses using probing classifiers, behavioral studies and test suites, and interactive visualizations. We will highlight not only the most commonly applied analysis methods, but also the specific limitations and shortcomings of current approaches, in order to inform participants where to focus future efforts.

1 Tutorial Description

Deep learning has transformed the NLP field and impacted the larger computational linguistics community. Neural networks have become the preferred modeling approach for various tasks, from language modeling, through morphological inflection and syntactic parsing, to machine translation, summarization, and reading comprehension.

The rise of neural networks is, however, stained by their opaque nature. In contrast to earlier approaches that made use of manually crafted features, it is more challenging to interpret the inner workings of neural network models, and explicate their behavior. Therefore, in the last few years, an increasingly large body of work has been devoted to the analysis and interpretation of neural network models in NLP.

The topic has so far been represented in two dedicated workshops (Blackbox 2018 and 2019) and was recently established as a track in the main *CL conferences. Due to these recent developments, methods for the analysis and interpretability of neural networks in NLP are so far lacking a common framework and methodology. Moreover, approaching the analysis of modern neural networks can be difficult for newcomers to the field, since it requires both a familiarity with recent work in neural NLP and with analysis methods which are not yet standardized. This tutorial aims to fill this gap and introduce the nascent field of interpretability and analysis of neural networks in NLP.

The tutorial will cover the main lines of analysis work, mostly drawing on the recent TACL survey by Belinkov and Glass (2019).[1] In particular, we will devote a large portion to work aiming to find linguistic information that is captured by neural networks, such as probing classifiers (Hupkes et al., 2018; Adi et al., 2017; Conneau et al., 2018a,b; Tenney et al., 2019b, inter alia), controlled behavior studies on language modelling (Gulordava et al., 2018; Linzen et al., 2016a; Marvin and Linzen, 2018) or inference tasks (Poliak et al., 2018a,b; White et al., 2017; Kim et al., 2019; McCoy et al., 2019; Ross and Pavlick, 2019), psycholinguistic methods (Ettinger et al., 2018; Chrupała and Alishahi, 2019), layerwise analyses (Peters et al., 2018; Tenney et al., 2019a), among other methods (Hewitt and Manning, 2019; Zhang

[1] A comprehensive bibliography is found in the accompanying website of the survey: `https://boknilev.github.io/nlp-analysis-methods/`.

Proceedings of the 58th Annual Meeting of the Association for Computational Linguistics, pages 1–5
July 5, 2020. ©2020 Association for Computational Linguistics
https://doi.org/10.18653/v1/P17

and Bowman, 2018; Shi et al., 2016). We will also present various interactive visualization methods such as neuron activations (Karpathy et al., 2015; Dalvi et al., 2019), attention mechanisms (Bahdanau et al., 2014; Strobelt et al., 2018), and saliency measures (Li et al., 2016; Murdoch et al., 2018; Arras et al., 2017), including a walkthrough on how to build a simple attention visualization. Next, we will discuss the construction and use of challenge sets for fine-grained evaluation in the context of different tasks (Conneau and Kiela, 2018; Wang et al., 2018; Isabelle and Kuhn, 2018; Sennrich, 2017, inter alia). Finally, we will review work on generating adversarial examples in NLP, focusing on the challenges brought upon by the discrete nature of textual input (Papernot et al., 2016b; Ebrahimi et al., 2018; Jia and Liang, 2017; Belinkov and Bisk, 2018, inter alia). A detailed outline is provided in Section 3.

Throughout the tutorial, we will highlight not only the most commonly applied analysis methods, but also the specific limitations and shortcomings of current approaches. By the end of the tutorial, participants will be better informed where to focus future research efforts.

2 Tutorial Type

This tutorial will cover cutting-edge research in interpretability and analysis of modern neural NLP models. The topic has not been previously covered in *CL tutorials.

3 Outline

1. Introduction
2. Structural Analyses
   (a) Methodology: Analysis by Probing Classifiers
   (b) Example Studies: Different Components and Linguistic Phenomena
   (c) Limitations
3. Behavioral Studies
   (a) Background on Test Suites and Challenge Sets
   (b) Types of Probing Tasks
   (c) Experimental Designs
   (d) Construction Methods
   (e) Languages
4. Interaction and Visualization
   (a) How Interaction can help and its limitations
   (b) Classification and Review of Related Efforts
   (c) Demo Walk-through: Simple Attention Visualization
   (d) Broader Perspectives and Opportunities
5. Other Methods
   (a) Generating Explanations
   (b) Psycholinguistic Methods
   (c) Testing on Formal Languages
6. Conclusion

4 Prerequisites

We would assume acquaintance with core linguistic concepts and basic knowledge of machine learning and neural networks, such as covered in most introductory NLP courses.

5 Reading List

In addition to the papers mentioned in this proposal, a comprehensive bibliography can be found in the following website: `https://boknilev.github.io/nlp-analysis-methods/`.

For trainees interested in reading important studies before the tutorial, we recommend the following: Belinkov and Glass (2019); Hupkes et al. (2018); Tenney et al. (2019b); Linzen et al. (2016b); Ettinger et al. (2018); Bahdanau et al. (2014); Li et al. (2016); Sennrich (2017); Papernot et al. (2016a); Ebrahimi et al. (2018).

6 Names and Affiliations

Yonatan Belinkov, Postdoctoral Fellow, Harvard University and MIT
email: `belinkov@seas.harvard.edu`
website: `http://people.csail.mit.edu/belinkov`

Yonatan Belinkov is a Postdoctoral Fellow at the Harvard School of Engineering and Applied Sciences (SEAS) and the MIT Computer Science and Artificial Intelligence Laboratory (CSAIL). His research interests are in interpretability and robustness of neural models of language. He has done previous work in machine translation, speech recognition, community question answering, and syntactic parsing. His research has been published at ACL, EMNLP, NAACL, CL, TACL, ICLR, and NeurIPS. His PhD dissertation at MIT analyzed internal language representations in deep learning models. He co-organized or co-organizes BlackboxNLP 2019, BlackboxNLP 2020, and the WMT 2019 machine translation robustness task, and serves as an area chair for the analysis and interpretability track at ACL and EMNLP 2020.

Sebastian Gehrmann, Research Scientist, Google AI
email: gehrmann@google.com
website: http://sebastiangehrmann.com

Sebastian is research scientist at Google AI. He received his PhD in 2020 from Harvard University. His research focuses on the development and evaluation of controllable and interpretable models for language generation. By applying methods from human-computer interaction and visualization to problems in NLP, he develops interactive interfaces that help with the interpretation and explanation of neural networks. His research has been published at ACL, NAACL, EMNLP, CHI, and IEEE VIS. He received an honorable mention at VAST 2018 and was nominated for ACL best demo 2019 for his work on interactive visualization tools. He co-organized INLG 2019 and served as an area chair in summarization for ACL 2020.

Ellie Pavlick, Assistant Professor of Computer Science, Brown University
email: ellie_pavlick@brown.edu
website: http://cs.brown.edu/people/epavlick

Ellie Pavlick is an Assistant Professor at Brown University and a Research Scientist at Google. She received her PhD in 2017 with her thesis on modeling compositional lexical semantics. Her current work focuses on computational models of semantics and pragmatics, with a focus on building cognitively-plausible representations. Her recent work has focused on "probing" distributional models in order to better understand the linguistic phenomena that are and are not encoded "for free" via language modelling. Her work has been published at ACL, NAACL, EMNLP, TACL, *SEM, and ICLR, including two best paper awards at *SEM 2016 and 2019. Ellie co-organized the 2018 JSALT summer workshop on building and evaluating general-purpose sentence representations. She also served as area chair for ACL's sentence-level semantics track.

References

Yossi Adi, Einat Kermany, Yonatan Belinkov, Ofer Lavi, and Yoav Goldberg. 2017. Fine-grained Analysis of Sentence Embeddings Using Auxiliary Prediction Tasks. In *International Conference on Learning Representations (ICLR)*.

Leila Arras, Franziska Horn, Grégoire Montavon, Klaus-Robert Müller, and Wojciech Samek. 2017. "What is relevant in a text document?": An interpretable machine learning approach. *PLOS ONE*, 12(8):1–23.

Dzmitry Bahdanau, Kyunghyun Cho, and Yoshua Bengio. 2014. Neural Machine Translation by Jointly Learning to Align and Translate. *arXiv preprint arXiv:1409.0473v7*.

Yonatan Belinkov and Yonatan Bisk. 2018. Synthetic and Natural Noise Both Break Neural Machine Translation. In *International Conference on Learning Representations (ICLR)*.

Yonatan Belinkov and James Glass. 2019. Analysis methods in neural language processing: A survey. *Transactions of the Association for Computational Linguistics*, 7:49–72.

Grzegorz Chrupała and Afra Alishahi. 2019. Correlating neural and symbolic representations of language. In *Proceedings of the 57th Annual Meeting of the Association for Computational Linguistics*, pages 2952–2962, Florence, Italy. Association for Computational Linguistics.

Alexis Conneau and Douwe Kiela. 2018. SentEval: An evaluation toolkit for universal sentence representations. In *Proceedings of the Eleventh International Conference on Language Resources and Evaluation (LREC-2018)*, Miyazaki, Japan. European Languages Resources Association (ELRA).

Alexis Conneau, Germán Kruszewski, Guillaume Lample, Loïc Barrault, and Marco Baroni. 2018a. What you can cram into a single $&!#* vector: Probing sentence embeddings for linguistic properties. In *Proceedings of the 56th Annual Meeting of the Association for Computational Linguistics (Volume 1: Long Papers)*, pages 2126–2136. Association for Computational Linguistics.

Alexis Conneau, German Kruszewski, Guillaume Lample, Loïc Barrault, and Marco Baroni. 2018b. What you can cram into a single $&!#* vector: Probing sentence embeddings for linguistic properties. In *Proceedings of the 56th Annual Meeting of* *the Association for Computational Linguistics (Volume 1: Long Papers)*, pages 2126–2136, Melbourne, Australia. Association for Computational Linguistics.

Fahim Dalvi, Avery Nortonsmith, D. Anthony Bau, Yonatan Belinkov, Hassan Sajjad, Nadir Durrani, and James Glass. 2019. NeuroX: A Toolkit for Analyzing Individual Neurons in Neural Networks. In *Proceedings of the Thirty-Third AAAI Conference on Artificial Intelligence (AAAI): Demonstrations Track.*

Javid Ebrahimi, Anyi Rao, Daniel Lowd, and Dejing Dou. 2018. HotFlip: White-Box Adversarial Examples for Text Classification. In *Proceedings of the 56th Annual Meeting of the Association for Computational Linguistics (Volume 2: Short Papers)*, pages 31–36. Association for Computational Linguistics.

Allyson Ettinger, Ahmed Elgohary, Colin Phillips, and Philip Resnik. 2018. Assessing composition in sentence vector representations. In *Proceedings of the 27th International Conference on Computational Linguistics*, pages 1790–1801, Santa Fe, New Mexico, USA. Association for Computational Linguistics.

Kristina Gulordava, Piotr Bojanowski, Edouard Grave, Tal Linzen, and Marco Baroni. 2018. Colorless green recurrent networks dream hierarchically. In *Proceedings of the 2018 Conference of the North American Chapter of the Association for Computational Linguistics: Human Language Technologies, Volume 1 (Long Papers)*, pages 1195–1205, New Orleans, Louisiana. Association for Computational Linguistics.

John Hewitt and Christopher D. Manning. 2019. A structural probe for finding syntax in word representations. In *Proceedings of the 2019 Conference of the North American Chapter of the Association for Computational Linguistics: Human Language Technologies, Volume 1 (Long and Short Papers)*, pages 4129–4138, Minneapolis, Minnesota. Association for Computational Linguistics.

Dieuwke Hupkes, Sara Veldhoen, and Willem Zuidema. 2018. Visualisation and 'diagnostic classifiers' reveal how recurrent and recursive neural networks process hierarchical structure. *Journal of Artificial Intelligence Research*, 61:907–926.

Pierre Isabelle and Roland Kuhn. 2018. A Challenge Set for French–¿ English Machine Translation. *arXiv preprint arXiv:1806.02725v2*.

Robin Jia and Percy Liang. 2017. Adversarial examples for evaluating reading comprehension systems. In *Proceedings of the 2017 Conference on Empirical Methods in Natural Language Processing*, pages 2021–2031. Association for Computational Linguistics.

Andrej Karpathy, Justin Johnson, and Fei-Fei Li. 2015. Visualizing and Understanding Recurrent Networks. *arXiv preprint arXiv:1506.02078v2*.

Najoung Kim, Roma Patel, Adam Poliak, Patrick Xia, Alex Wang, Tom McCoy, Ian Tenney, Alexis Ross, Tal Linzen, Benjamin Van Durme, Samuel R. Bowman, and Ellie Pavlick. 2019. Probing what different NLP tasks teach machines about function word comprehension. In *Proceedings of the Eighth Joint Conference on Lexical and Computational Semantics (*SEM 2019)*, pages 235–249, Minneapolis, Minnesota. Association for Computational Linguistics.

Jiwei Li, Will Monroe, and Dan Jurafsky. 2016. Understanding Neural Networks through Representation Erasure. *arXiv preprint arXiv:1612.08220v3*.

Tal Linzen, Emmanuel Dupoux, and Yoav Goldberg. 2016a. Assessing the ability of LSTMs to learn syntax-sensitive dependencies. *Transactions of the Association for Computational Linguistics*, 4:521–535.

Tal Linzen, Emmanuel Dupoux, and Yoav Goldberg. 2016b. Assessing the Ability of LSTMs to Learn Syntax-Sensitive Dependencies. *Transactions of the Association for Computational Linguistics*, 4:521–535.

Rebecca Marvin and Tal Linzen. 2018. Targeted syntactic evaluation of language models. In *Proceedings of the 2018 Conference on Empirical Methods in Natural Language Processing*, pages 1192–1202, Brussels, Belgium. Association for Computational Linguistics.

Tom McCoy, Ellie Pavlick, and Tal Linzen. 2019. Right for the wrong reasons: Diagnosing syntactic heuristics in natural language inference. In *Proceedings of the 57th Annual Meeting of the Association for Computational Linguistics*, pages 3428–3448, Florence, Italy. Association for Computational Linguistics.

W. James Murdoch, Peter J. Liu, and Bin Yu. 2018. Beyond Word Importance: Contextual Decomposition to Extract Interactions from LSTMs. In *International Conference on Learning Representations.*

Nicolas Papernot, Patrick McDaniel, and Ian Goodfellow. 2016a. Transferability in Machine Learning: From Phenomena to Black-Box Attacks using Adversarial Samples. *arXiv preprint arXiv:1605.07277v1*.

Nicolas Papernot, Patrick McDaniel, Ananthram Swami, and Richard Harang. 2016b. Crafting Adversarial Input Sequences for Recurrent Neural Networks. In *Military Communications Conference (MILCOM)*, pages 49–54. IEEE.

Matthew Peters, Mark Neumann, Luke Zettlemoyer, and Wen-tau Yih. 2018. Dissecting contextual word embeddings: Architecture and representation.

In *Proceedings of the 2018 Conference on Empirical Methods in Natural Language Processing*, pages 1499–1509, Brussels, Belgium. Association for Computational Linguistics.

Adam Poliak, Yonatan Belinkov, James Glass, and Benjamin Van Durme. 2018a. On the evaluation of semantic phenomena in neural machine translation using natural language inference. In *Proceedings of the 2018 Conference of the North American Chapter of the Association for Computational Linguistics: Human Language Technologies, Volume 2 (Short Papers)*, pages 513–523, New Orleans, Louisiana. Association for Computational Linguistics.

Adam Poliak, Aparajita Haldar, Rachel Rudinger, J. Edward Hu, Ellie Pavlick, Aaron Steven White, and Benjamin Van Durme. 2018b. Collecting diverse natural language inference problems for sentence representation evaluation. In *Proceedings of the 2018 Conference on Empirical Methods in Natural Language Processing*, pages 67–81, Brussels, Belgium. Association for Computational Linguistics.

Alexis Ross and Ellie Pavlick. 2019. How well do nli models capture verb veridicality? In *Proceedings of the 2016 Conference on Empirical Methods in Natural Language Processing*, Hong Kong, China. Association for Computational Linguistics.

Rico Sennrich. 2017. How Grammatical is Character-level Neural Machine Translation? Assessing MT Quality with Contrastive Translation Pairs. In *Proceedings of the 15th Conference of the European Chapter of the Association for Computational Linguistics: Volume 2, Short Papers*, pages 376–382. Association for Computational Linguistics.

Xing Shi, Inkit Padhi, and Kevin Knight. 2016. Does string-based neural MT learn source syntax? In *Proceedings of the 2016 Conference on Empirical Methods in Natural Language Processing*, pages 1526–1534, Austin, Texas. Association for Computational Linguistics.

Hendrik Strobelt, Sebastian Gehrmann, Michael Behrisch, Adam Perer, Hanspeter Pfister, and Alexander M Rush. 2018. Seq2seq-vis: A visual debugging tool for sequence-to-sequence models. *IEEE transactions on visualization and computer graphics*, 25(1):353–363.

Ian Tenney, Dipanjan Das, and Ellie Pavlick. 2019a. BERT rediscovers the classical NLP pipeline. In *Proceedings of the 57th Annual Meeting of the Association for Computational Linguistics*, pages 4593–4601, Florence, Italy. Association for Computational Linguistics.

Ian Tenney, Patrick Xia, Berlin Chen, Alex Wang, Adam Poliak, R Thomas McCoy, Najoung Kim, Benjamin Van Durme, Sam Bowman, Dipanjan Das, and Ellie Pavlick. 2019b. What do you learn from context? probing for sentence structure in contextualized word representations. In *International Conference on Learning Representations*.

Alex Wang, Amapreet Singh, Julian Michael, Felix Hill, Omer Levy, and Samuel R. Bowman. 2018. GLUE: A Multi-Task Benchmark and Analysis Platform for Natural Language Understanding. *arXiv preprint arXiv:1804.07461v1*.

Aaron Steven White, Pushpendre Rastogi, Kevin Duh, and Benjamin Van Durme. 2017. Inference is everything: Recasting semantic resources into a unified evaluation framework. In *Proceedings of the Eighth International Joint Conference on Natural Language Processing (Volume 1: Long Papers)*, pages 996–1005, Taipei, Taiwan. Asian Federation of Natural Language Processing.

Kelly Zhang and Samuel Bowman. 2018. Language modeling teaches you more than translation does: Lessons learned through auxiliary syntactic task analysis. In *Proceedings of the 2018 EMNLP Workshop BlackboxNLP: Analyzing and Interpreting Neural Networks for NLP*, pages 359–361, Brussels, Belgium. Association for Computational Linguistics.

Integrating Ethics into the NLP Curriculum

Emily M. Bender
University of Washington
ebender@uw.edu

Dirk Hovy
Bocconi University
dirk.hovy@unibocconi.it

Xanda Schofield
Harvey Mudd College
xanda@cs.hmc.edu

1 Description

As NLP technology becomes more ubiquitous, it has ever more impact on the lives of people all around the world. As a field, we have become increasingly aware that we have a responsibility to evaluate the effects of our research and mitigate harmful outcomes. This is true for both researchers and developers in universities, government labs, and industry. However, without experience of how to productively engage with the many ethical conundrums in NLP, it is easy to become overwhelmed and remain inactive. To raise awareness among future NLP practitioners and prevent inertia in the field, we need to place ethics in the curriculum for all NLP students—not as an elective, but as a core part of their education. Though ethical considerations are achieving new currency in NLP, similar issues have been under consideration for decades, if not centuries, in other fields, and there are robust existing practices for approaching these problems. The difference is that there is no agreed-upon way to engage with them in our field.

Our goal in this tutorial is to empower NLP researchers and practitioners with tools and resources to teach others about how to ethically apply NLP techniques. Our tutorial will present both high-level strategies for developing an ethics-oriented curriculum, based on experience and best practices, as well as specific sample exercises that can be brought to a classroom.[1] We plan to make this a highly interactive work session culminating in a shared online resource page that pools lesson plans, assignments, exercise ideas, reading suggestions, and ideas from the attendees. Though the tutorial will focus particularly on examples for college classrooms, we believe the ideas can extend to company-internal workshops or tutorials in a variety of organizations.

We consider three primary topics with our session that frequently underlie ethical issues in NLP research:

1. **Dual Use**: Learning how to anticipate how a developed technology could be repurposed for harmful or negative results, and designing systems so that they do not inadvertently cause harm.

2. **Bias**: Understanding the different ways in which bias interacts with language data, including over- and under-sampling of different populations as well as the effects of human bias expressed in language; building less biased datasets and debiasing trained models; strategies for matching appropriate training data to a given use case.

3. **Privacy**: Protecting the privacy of speakers/writers of text used in the construction or evaluation of a new NLP technology.

In this setting, a key lesson is that there is no single approach to ethical NLP: each project requires thoughtful consideration about what steps can be taken to best support people affected by that project. However, we can learn (and teach) what kinds of issues to be aware of and what kinds of strategies are available for mitigating harm. To teach this process, we apply and promote interactive exercises that provide an opportunity to ideate, discuss, and reflect. We plan to facilitate this in a way that encourages positive discussion, emphasizing the creation of ideas for the future instead of negative opinions of previous work.

2 Type of tutorial

Introductory. Though this is a topic of importance to the NLP community internally, it relies

[1]The specific exercises we propose include ones that have been field-tested.

Proceedings of the 58th Annual Meeting of the Association for Computational Linguistics, pages 6–9
July 5, 2020. ©2020 Association for Computational Linguistics
https://doi.org/10.18653/v1/P17

on existing expertise from both pedagogical and philosophical work, and it is not meant to depend on any particular research area of NLP. However, we do believe the content of this workshop also explores questions not fully answered in our field about concrete best practices in the specific context of NLP courses.

A note on interactivity: The proposed format of this tutorial is different from many past introductory tutorials, in the sense that it relies heavily on participation as part of the instruction. However, we believe this is a necessary part of the format of this tutorial for several reasons:

- Because our tutorial is focused on pedagogy, it makes sense to use effective and equitable pedagogical classroom techniques in it. Interactivity through active or cooperative learning (Slavin, 1980; Johnson and Johnson, 2008) and guided discovery-based learning (Alfieri et al., 2011) are proven to enable students to learn more effectively across diverse classrooms, and our design models this.

- The outcome of this tutorial is one focused on training and professional development, which comes with practice. In the same way one might encourage developing a sample neural network in a tutorial on deep learning, we encourage performing steps of educational practice to develop skills to then use in our lives as instructors.

- While there exists literature in ethics pedagogy and ethics in NLP, there do not exist large pools of resources and papers to refer when designing a course, but instead only a small collection of syllabi for ethics in machine learning/NLP courses. An interactive tutorial format allows us to use the learning experiences of our participants as a starting point to construct a more centralized pool of resources from which faculty and educators in NLP can draw.

3 Outline

1. Introduction, background, motivation [10m]

2. Core concepts and terminology, and warm up exercises. [50m] We will have the participants discuss what motivates them and core concepts of ethics and pedagogy that might be useful in the subsequent ideation.

3. Big class exercise I [55m] (5 minutes intro, 35 minutes doing the exercise with the group, 10 minutes talking about how to teach it). The exercises in this set are centered around thinking through how systems behave in the world. There will be a separate exercise for each of the three groups: dual use, bias, and privacy.

   Dual Use A student approaches you because they want to explore gendered language in the LGBTQ community. They are very engaged in the community themselves and have access to data. Their plan is to write a text classification tool that distinguishes LGBTQ from heterosexual language. What do you tell the student?

   Bias Pick an application of speech/language technology, determine what kind of training data is typically used for it (whose language? recorded when/where/how?). Next, imagine real world use cases for this technology. What speaker groups would come in contact with the system? If their language differs from substantially from the training data, what would the failure mode of the system be and what would the real-world impacts of that failure be? How could systems, their training data or documentation be designed to be robust to this kind of problem?

   Privacy Consider a simple Naive Bayes classifier trained on a subset of 20 Newsgroups using word frequencies as features. For five sample messages, could you tell whether or not they were included in the subset? How would you check? How certain could you be?

4. Big class exercise II [55m] (5 minutes intro, 25 minutes refining the exercise, 25 minutes talking about how to teach it). The exercises in this set involve building a system and observing its behavior.

   Dual Use (1) An ACL submission claims to be able to undo ciphers used by dissenters on social media. Who benefits from this? Is it better to release it in a peer-reviewed venue than to not know it? (2) You develop a tool that can detect depression with high accuracy.

Why, or why not, should you release it as an app?

Bias Taking inspiration from Speer (2017b), build a sentiment analysis system over restaurant reviews using different sources of training data for word embeddings. What kind of biases can be observed in system behavior for different types of cuisine? What patterns in language use in the underlying training data are responsible? What kinds of analogous problems can arise in other systems that use word embeddings as input?

Privacy Design a small search engine around an inverted index that uses random integer noise from a two-sided geometric distribution (Ghosh et al., 2012) to shape which queries are retrieved. Analyze how much this changes the search results with different noise levels. Are there systematic changes?

5. Wrap up [20m]: big points, reflections from people, where to find resources and keep talking

4 Prerequisites

This tutorial is meant to be accessible to anyone actively working with NLP and either currently teaching, interested in teaching, or interested in informal instruction outside of university contexts.

5 Reading List

We recommend the following short readings to get a sense of the kinds of issues we will be approaching:

- Dual Use: Ehni 2008
- Bias: Speer 2017a
- Privacy: Coavoux et al. 2018

In addition, we recommend the following papers for a sense of what can be learned from other fields:

- Value scenarios, a technique from value sensitive design: Nathan et al. 2007
- A history of notions of fairness in education and hiring: Hutchinson and Mitchell 2019
- Disparate impact: Feldman et al. 2015

Participants are encouraged to have read at least some of these papers ahead of time, but familiarity with all of them will not be assumed.

6 Instructors

Emily M. Bender
University of Washington
ebender@uw.edu
faculty.washington.edu/ebender

Emily M. Bender is a Professor of Linguistics and Adjunct Professor of Computer Science and Engineering at the University of Washington. Her research interests include computational semantics, grammar engineering, computational linguistic typology, and ethics in NLP. She is the Faculty Director of UW's Professional Masters in Computational Linguistics (CLMS) and has been engaged with integrating ethics into the CLMS curriculum since 2016. She co-organized the first EthNLP workshop. Her first publication in this area is the TACL paper "Data Statements for NLP: Toward Mitigating System Bias and Enabling Better Science" (Bender and Friedman, 2018) and she has been an invited speaker at workshops and panels related to ethics and NLP (or AI more broadly) at the Taskar Memorial Event (UW, March 2018), The Future of Artificial Intelligence: Language, Ethics, Technology (Cambridge, March 2019), West Coast NLP (Facebook, September 2019), Machine Learning Competitions for All (NeurIPS, December 2019) and AAAS (Seattle, February 2020).

Xanda Schofield
Harvey Mudd College
xanda@cs.hmc.edu
www.cs.hmc.edu/~xanda

Xanda Schofield is an Assistant Professor of Computer Science at Harvey Mudd College. Her work focuses on the practical aspects of using distributional semantic models for analysis of real-world datasets, with problems ranging from understanding the consequences of data pre-processing on model inference (Schofield and Mimno, 2016; Schofield et al., 2017) to enforcing text privacy for these models (Schein et al., 2018). She also is interested in pedagogy at this intersection, having co-developed a Text Mining for History and Literature course at Cornell University with David Mimno. She is currently focusing pedagogical efforts on how to introduce considerations of ethics and bias into other courses such as Algorithms.

Dirk Hovy
Bocconi University
dirk.hovy@unibocconi.it
www.dirkhovy.com

Dirk Hovy is an Associate Professor of Computer Science in the Department of Marketing at Bocconi University in Milan, Italy. His research focuses on how social dimensions influence language and in turn NLP models, as well as on questions of bias and fairness. He strives to integrate sociolinguistic knowledge into NLP models to counteract demographic bias. Dirk has written on ethics and bias in NLP (Hovy and Spruit, 2016), co-organized two editions of the EthNLP workshops and one of the abusive language workshop, and was an invited speaker on panels on ethics at NAACL 2018 and SLT 2018. He is teaching a related tutorial (on ethics and biases) at CLiC-IT in November 2019.

References

Louis Alfieri, Patricia J Brooks, Naomi J Aldrich, and Harriet R Tenenbaum. 2011. Does discovery-based instruction enhance learning? *Journal of educational psychology*, 103(1):1.

Emily M. Bender and Batya Friedman. 2018. Data Statements for NLP: Toward Mitigating System Bias and Enabling Better Science. *Transactions of the Association for Computational Linguistics*, 6.

Maximin Coavoux, Shashi Narayan, and Shay B. Cohen. 2018. Privacy-preserving neural representations of text. In *Proceedings of the 2018 Conference on Empirical Methods in Natural Language Processing*, pages 1–10. Association for Computational Linguistics.

Hans-Jörg Ehni. 2008. Dual use and the ethical responsibility of scientists. *Archivum immunologiae et therapiae experimentalis*, 56(3):147.

Michael Feldman, Sorelle A Friedler, John Moeller, Carlos Scheidegger, and Suresh Venkatasubramanian. 2015. Certifying and removing disparate impact. In *Proceedings of the 21th ACM SIGKDD International Conference on Knowledge Discovery and Data Mining*, pages 259–268. ACM.

Arpita Ghosh, Tim Roughgarden, and Mukund Sundararajan. 2012. Universally utility-maximizing privacy mechanisms. *SIAM Journal on Computing*, 41(6):1673–1693.

Dirk Hovy and Shannon L. Spruit. 2016. The social impact of natural language processing. In *Proceedings of the 54th Annual Meeting of the Association for Computational Linguistics (Volume 2: Short Papers)*, pages 591–598. Association for Computational Linguistics.

Ben Hutchinson and Margaret Mitchell. 2019. 50 years of test (un)fairness: Lessons for machine learning. In *Proceedings of FAT* 19: Conference on Fairness, Accountability, and Transparency (FAT* 19)*, volume abs/1811.10104, New York. ACM.

Roger T Johnson and David W Johnson. 2008. Active learning: Cooperation in the classroom. *The annual report of educational psychology in Japan*, 47:29–30.

Lisa P. Nathan, Predrag V. Klasnja, and Batya Friedman. 2007. Value scenarios: A technique for envisioning systemic effects of new technologies. In *CHI'07 Extended Abstracts on Human Factors in Computing Systems*, pages 2585–2590. ACM.

Aaron Schein, Zhiwei Steven Wu, Alexandra Schofield, Mingyuan Zhou, and Hanna Wallach. 2018. Locally private bayesian inference for count models. *arXiv preprint arXiv:1803.08471*.

Alexandra Schofield, Måns Magnusson, and David Mimno. 2017. Pulling out the stops: Rethinking stopword removal for topic models. In *Proceedings of the 15th Conference of the European Chapter of the Association for Computational Linguistics: Volume 2, Short Papers*, pages 432–436.

Alexandra Schofield and David Mimno. 2016. Comparing apples to apple: The effects of stemmers on topic models. *Transactions of the Association for Computational Linguistics*, 4:287–300.

Robert E Slavin. 1980. Cooperative learning. *Review of educational research*, 50(2):315–342.

Robyn Speer. 2017a. Conceptnet numberbatch 17.04: better, less-stereotyped word vectors. Blog post, https://blog.conceptnet.io/2017/04/24/conceptnet-numberbatch-17-04-better-less-stereotyped-word-vectors/, accessed 15 January 2019.

Robyn Speer. 2017b. How to make a racist AI without really trying. Blog post, http://blog.conceptnet.io/posts/2017/how-to-make-a-racist-ai-without-really-trying/, accessed 15 January 2019.

Achieving Common Ground in Multi-modal Dialogue

Malihe Alikhani
Computer Science
Rutgers University
malihe.alikhani@rutgers.edu

Matthew Stone
Computer Science
Rutgers University
matthew.stone@rutgers.edu

1 Description

All communication aims at achieving common ground (grounding): interlocutors can work together effectively only with mutual beliefs about what the state of the world is, about what their goals are, and about how they plan to make their goals a reality (Clark et al., 1991). Computational dialogue research, in particular, has a long history of influential work on how implemented systems can achieve common ground with human users, from formal results on grounding actions in conversation (Traum, 1994) to machine learning results on how best to fold confirmation actions into dialogue flow (Levin et al., 1998; Walker, 2000). Such classic results, however, offer scant guidance to the design of grounding modules and behaviors in cutting-edge systems, which increasingly combine multiple communication modalities, address complex tasks, and include the possibility for lightweight practical action interleaved with communication. This tutorial is premised on the idea that it's time to revisit work on grounding in human–human conversation, particularly Brennan's general and important characterization of grounding as seeking and providing evidence of mutual understanding (Brennan, 1990), in light of the opportunities and challenges of multi-modal settings such as human–robot interaction.

In this tutorial, we focus on three main topic areas: 1) grounding in human-human communication; 2) grounding in dialogue systems; and 3) grounding in multi-modal interactive systems, including image-oriented conversations and human-robot interactions. We highlight a number of achievements of recent computational research in coordinating complex content, show how these results lead to rich and challenging opportunities for doing grounding in more flexible and powerful ways, and canvass relevant insights from the literature on human–human conversation. We expect that the tutorial will be of interest to researchers in dialogue systems, computational semantics and cognitive modeling, and hope that it will catalyze research and system building that more directly explores the creative, strategic ways conversational agents might be able to seek and offer evidence about their understanding of their interlocutors.

A: A green bike with tan handlebars. B: Got it (Manuvinakurike et al., 2017)

A: The green cup is called Bill. B: Ok, the green cup is Bill. [point to the inferred object] (Liu and Chai, 2015)

Figure 1: Examples of the generation and interpretation of grounded referring expressions in multimodal interactive settings. Grounding is making sure that the listener understands what the speaker said.

Grounding in human-human communication. Clark et al. (1991) argued that communication is accomplished in two phases. In the presentation phase, the speaker presents signals intended to specify the content of the contributions. In the second phase, the participants work together to establish mutual beliefs that serve the purposes of the conversation. The two phases together constitute a unit of communication–*contributions*. Clark and Krych (2004) show how this model applies to coordinated action, while Stone and Stojnić (2015) applies the model to text-and-video presentations.

Proceedings of the 58th Annual Meeting of the Association for Computational Linguistics, pages 10–15
July 5, 2020.
https://doi.org/10.18653/v1/P17

Coherence is key.

Grounding in dialogue systems. Computer systems achieve grounding mechanistically by ensuring they get attention and feedback from their users, tracking user state, and planning actions with reinforcement learning to resolve problematic situations. We will review techniques for maintaining engagement (Sidner et al., 2005; Bohus and Horvitz, 2014; Foster et al., 2017) and problems that arises in joint attention (Kontogiorgos et al., 2018) and turn taking such as incremental interpretation (DeVault and Stone, 2004; DeVault et al., 2011), ambiguity resolution (DeVault and Stone, 2009) and learning flexible dialogue management policies (Henderson et al., 2005). Similar questions have been studied in the context of instruction games (Perera et al., 2018; Thomason et al., 2019; Suhr and Artzi, 2018), and interactive tutoring systems (Yu et al., 2016; Wiggins et al., 2019).

Grounding in multi-modal systems. Multimodal systems offer the ability to use signals such as nodding, certain hand gestures and gazing at a speaker to communicate meaning and contribute to establishing common ground (Mavridis, 2015). However, multi-modal grounding is more than just using pointing to clarify. Multi-modal systems have diverse opportunities to demonstrate understanding. For example, recent work has aimed to bridge vision, interactive learning, and natural language understanding through language learning tasks based on natural images (Zhang et al., 2018; Kazemzadeh et al., 2014; De Vries et al., 2017a; Kim et al., 2020). The work on visual dialogue games (Geman et al., 2015) brings new resources and models for generating referring expression for referents in images (Suhr et al., 2019; Shekhar et al., 2018), visually grounded spoken language communication (Roy, 2002; Gkatzia et al., 2015), and captioning (Levinboim et al., 2019; Alikhani and Stone, 2019), which can be used creatively to demonstrate how a system understand a user. Figure 1 shows two examples of models that understand and generate referring expressions in multimodal settings.

Similarly, robots can demostrate how they understand a task by carring it out—in research on interactive task learning in human-robot interaction (Zarrieß and Schlangen, 2018; Carlmeyer et al., 2018) as well as embodied agents perform-

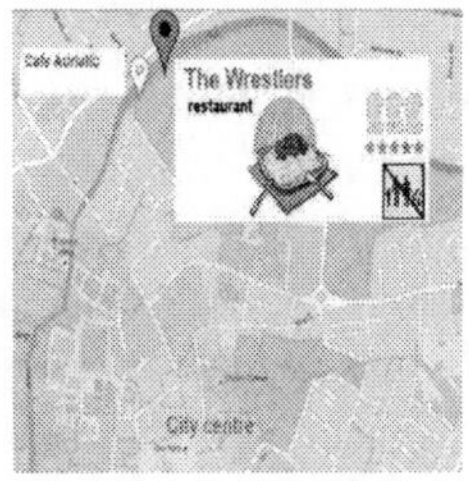

Show me a restaurant by the river, serving pasta/Italian food, highly rated and expensive, not child-friendly, located near Cafe Adriatic. (Novikova et al., 2016)

Crystal Island, an interactive narrative-centered virtual learning environment (Rowe et al., 2008)

Figure 2: Content and medium affect grounding. This figure shows two examples of interactive multimodal dialogue systems.

ing interactive tasks (Gordon et al., 2018; Das et al., 2018) in physically simulated environments (Anderson et al., 2018; Tan and Bansal, 2018) often drawing on the successes of deep learning and reinforcement learning (Branavan et al., 2009; Liu and Chai, 2015). A lesson that can be learned from this line of research is that one main factor that affects grounding is the choice of medium of communication. Thus, researchers have developed different techniques and methods for data collection and modeling of multimodal communication (Alikhani et al., 2019; Novikova et al., 2016). Figure 2 shows two example resources that were put together using crowdsourcing and virtual reality systems. We will discuss the strengths and shortcomings of these methods.

We pay special attention to non-verbal grounding in languages beyond English, including German (Han and Schlangen, 2018), Swedish (Kontogiorgos, 2017), Japanese (Endrass et al., 2013; Nakano et al., 2003), French (Lemaignan and Alami, 2013; Steels, 2001), Italian (Borghi and Cangelosi, 2014; Taylor et al., 1986), Spanish (Kery et al., 2019), Russian (Janda, 1988), and American sign language (Emmorey and Casey, 1995). These investigations often describe important language-dependent characteristics and cultural differences in studying non-verbal grounding.

Grounding in end-to-end language & vision systems. With current advances in neural modelling and the availability of large pretrained models in language and vision, multi-modal interaction often is enabled by neural end-to-end architectures with multimodal encodings, e.g. by answering questions abut visual scenes (Antol et al., 2015; Das et al., 2017). It is argued that these shared representations help to ground word meanings. In this tutorial, we will discuss how this type of lexical grounding relates to grounding in dialogue from a theoretical perspective (Larsson, 2018), as well as within different interactive application scenarios – ranging from interactively identifying an object (De Vries et al., 2017b) to dialogue-based learning of word meanings (Yu et al., 2016). We then critically review existing datasets and shared tasks and showcase some of the shortcomings of current vision and language models, e.g. (Agarwal et al., 2018). In contrast to previous ACL tutorials on Multimodal Learning and Reasoning, we will concentrate on identifying different grounding phenomena as identified in the first part of this tutorial.

2 Outline

We begin by discussing grounding in human-human communication (~20 min). After that, we discuss the role of grounding in spoken dialogue systems (~30 min) and visually grounded interactions including grounding visual explanations in images and multimodal language grounding for human-robot collaboration (~90 min). We then survey methods for developing and testing multimodal systems to study non-verbal grounding (~20 min). We follow this by describing common solution concepts and barrier problems that cross application domains and interaction types (~20 min).

3 Prerequisites and reading list

The tutorial will be self-contained. For further readings, we recommend the following publications that are central to the non-verbal grounding framework as of late 2019:

1. Grounding in communication, Herb Clark and Susan Brennan. (Clark et al., 1991)
2. Meaning and demonstration by Una Stojnic and Matthew Stone (Stone and Stojnić, 2015)
3. Using Reinforcement Learning to Model Incrementality in a Fast-Paced Dialogue Game, Ramesh Manuvinakurike, David DeVault and Kallirroi Georgila. (Manuvinakurike et al., 2017)
4. Language to Action: Towards Interactive Task Learning with Physical Agents, Joyce Y. Chai by Joyce Y. Chai et al.(Chai et al., 2018)
5. It's Not What You Do, It's How You Do It: Grounding Uncertainty for a Simple Robot, Julian Hough and David Schlangen. (Hough and Schlangen, 2017)
6. Learning Effective Multimodal Dialogue Strategies from Wizard-of-Oz Data: Bootstrapping and Evaluation rieser-lemon by Verena Rieser and Oliver Lemon. (Rieser and Lemon, 2008)
7. A survey of nonverbal signaling methods for non-humanoid robots by Elizabeth Cha et al. (Cha et al., 2018)
8. The Devil is in the Details: A Magnifying Glass for the GuessWhich Visual Dialogue Game by Alberto Testoni et al. (Testoni et al., 2019)

4 Authors

Malihe Alikhani is a 5th year Ph.D. student in the department of Computer sSience at Rutgers University `ma1195@cs.rutgers.edu`, advised by Prof. Matthew Stone. She is pursuing a certificate in cognitive science through the Rutgers Center for Cognitive Science and holds a BA and MA in Mathematics. Her research aims at teaching machines to understand and generate multimodal communication. She is the recipient of the fellowship award for excellence in computation and data sciences from Rutgers Discovery Informatics Institute in 2018 and the Anita Berg student fellowship in 2019. Before joining Rutgers, she was a lecturer and an adjunct professor of Mathematics and Statistics for a year at San Diego State University and San Diego Mesa College. She has served as the program committee of ACL, NAACL, EMNLP, AAAI, ICRL, ICMI, and INLG and is currently the associate editor of the Mental Note Journal. email: `ma1195@cs.rutgers.edu`, webpage: `www.malihealikhani.com`

Matthew Stone is professor and chair in the Department of Computer Science at Rutgers University; he holds a joint appointment in the Rutgers Center for Cognitive Science. His research focuses on discourse, dialogue and natural language generation; he is particularly interested in leveraging semantics to make interactive systems easier to build and more human-like in their behavior. He was program co-chair for NAACL 2007, general co-chair for SIGDIAL 2014. He has also served as program co-chair for INLG and IWCS, as an information officer for SIGSEM, and on the editorial board for Computational Linguistics. email: `mdstone@cs.rutgers.edu`, website: `www.cs.rutgers.edu/~mdstone/`

Acknowledgments

Preparation of this tutorial was supported in part by the DATA-INSPIRE Institute at Rutgers `http://robotics.cs.rutgers.edu/data-inspire/` under NSF HDR TRIPODS award CCF-1934924. We gratefully acknowledge the effort of Professor Verena Rieser of Heriot-Watt University, who discussed the tutorial with us extensively but was ultimately unable to participate due to the disruption of COVID-19.

References

Shubham Agarwal, Ondřej Dušek, Ioannis Konstas, and Verena Rieser. 2018. Improving context modelling in multimodal dialogue generation. In *Proceedings of the 11th International Conference on Natural Language Generation*.

Malihe Alikhani, Sreyasi Nag Chowdhury, Gerard de Melo, and Matthew Stone. 2019. Cite: A corpus of image-text discourse relations. In *Proceedings of the 2019 Conference of the North American Chapter of the Association for Computational Linguistics: Human Language Technologies, Volume 1 (Long and Short Papers)*, pages 570–575.

Malihe Alikhani and Matthew Stone. 2019. caption as a coherence relation: Evidence and implications. In *Proceedings of the Second Workshop on Shortcomings in Vision and Language*, pages 58–67.

Peter Anderson, Qi Wu, Damien Teney, Jake Bruce, Mark Johnson, Niko Sünderhauf, Ian Reid, Stephen Gould, and Anton van den Hengel. 2018. Vision-and-language navigation: Interpreting visually-grounded navigation instructions in real environments. In *Proceedings of the IEEE Conference on Computer Vision and Pattern Recognition*, pages 3674–3683.

Stanislaw Antol, Aishwarya Agrawal, Jiasen Lu, Margaret Mitchell, Dhruv Batra, C Lawrence Zitnick, and Devi Parikh. 2015. VQA: Visual question answering. In *ICCV*.

Dan Bohus and Eric Horvitz. 2014. Managing human-robot engagement with forecasts and... um... hesitations. In *Proceedings of the 16th international conference on multimodal interaction*. ACM.

Anna M Borghi and Angelo Cangelosi. 2014. Action and language integration: From humans to cognitive robots. *Topics in cognitive science*, 6(3):344–358.

Satchuthananthavale RK Branavan, Harr Chen, Luke S Zettlemoyer, and Regina Barzilay. 2009. Reinforcement learning for mapping instructions to actions. In *Proceedings of the Joint Conference of the 47th Annual Meeting of the ACL*, pages 82–90.

Susan E. Brennan. 1990. *Seeking and Providing Evidence for Mutual Understanding*. Ph.D. thesis, Stanford University.

Birte Carlmeyer, Simon Betz, Petra Wagner, Britta Wrede, and David Schlangen. 2018. The hesitating robot-implementation and first impressions. In *Companion of the 2018 ACM/IEEE International Conference on Human-Robot Interaction*.

Elizabeth Cha, Yunkyung Kim, Terrence Fong, Maja J Mataric, et al. 2018. A survey of nonverbal signaling methods for non-humanoid robots. *Foundations and Trends® in Robotics*, 6(4):211–323.

Joyce Y Chai, Qiaozi Gao, Lanbo She, Shaohua Yang, Sari Saba-Sadiya, and Guangyue Xu. 2018. Language to action: Towards interactive task learning with physical agents. In *AAMAS*, page 6.

Herbert H Clark, Susan E Brennan, et al. 1991. Grounding in communication. *Perspectives on socially shared cognition*, 13(1991):127–149.

Herbert H. Clark and Meredyth A. Krych. 2004. Speaking while monitoring addressees for understanding. *Journal of Memory and Language*, 50:62–81.

Abhishek Das, Samyak Datta, Georgia Gkioxari, Stefan Lee, Devi Parikh, and Dhruv Batra. 2018. Embodied question answering. In *Proceedings of the IEEE Conference on Computer Vision and Pattern Recognition Workshops*, pages 2054–2063.

Abhishek Das, Satwik Kottur, Khushi Gupta, Avi Singh, Deshraj Yadav, José MF Moura, Devi Parikh, and Dhruv Batra. 2017. Visual dialog. In *CVPR*.

Harm De Vries, Florian Strub, Sarath Chandar, Olivier Pietquin, Hugo Larochelle, and Aaron Courville. 2017a. Guesswhat?! visual object discovery through multi-modal dialogue. In *Proceedings of the IEEE Conference on Computer Vision and Pattern Recognition*.

Harm De Vries, Florian Strub, Sarath Chandar, Olivier Pietquin, Hugo Larochelle, and Aaron Courville. 2017b. Guesswhat?! visual object discovery through multi-modal dialogue. In *CVPR*.

David DeVault, Kenji Sagae, and David Traum. 2011. Incremental interpretation and prediction of utterance meaning for interactive dialogue. *Dialogue & Discourse*, 2(1):143–170.

David DeVault and Matthew Stone. 2004. Interpreting vague utterances in context. In *Proceedings of the 20th international conference on Computational Linguistics*, page 1247. Association for Computational Linguistics.

David DeVault and Matthew Stone. 2009. Learning to interpret utterances using dialogue history. In *Proceedings of the 12th Conference of the European Chapter of the Association for Computational Linguistics*.

Karen Emmorey and Shannon Casey. 1995. A comparison of spatial language in english & american sign language. *Sign Language Studies*, 88(1):255–288.

Birgit Endrass, Elisabeth André, Matthias Rehm, and Yukiko Nakano. 2013. Investigating culture-related aspects of behavior for virtual characters. *Autonomous Agents and Multi-Agent Systems*.

Mary Ellen Foster, Andre Gaschler, and Manuel Giuliani. 2017. Automatically classifying user engagement for dynamic multi-party human–robot interaction. *International Journal of Social Robotics*.

Donald Geman, Stuart Geman, Neil Hallonquist, and Laurent Younes. 2015. Visual turing test for computer vision systems. *Proceedings of the National Academy of Sciences*, 112(12):3618–3623.

Dimitra Gkatzia, Amanda Cercas Curry, Verena Rieser, and Oliver Lemon. 2015. A game-based setup for data collection and task-based evaluation of uncertain information presentation. In *Proceedings of the 15th European Workshop on Natural Language Generation (ENLG)*.

Daniel Gordon, Aniruddha Kembhavi, Mohammad Rastegari, Joseph Redmon, Dieter Fox, and Ali Farhadi. 2018. Iqa: Visual question answering in interactive environments. In *Proceedings of the IEEE Conference on Computer Vision and Pattern Recognition*, pages 4089–4098.

Ting Han and David Schlangen. 2018. A corpus of natural multimodal spatial scene descriptions. In *Proceedings of the Eleventh International Conference on Language Resources and Evaluation (LREC-2018)*.

James Henderson, Oliver Lemon, and Kallirroi Georgila. 2005. Hybrid reinforcement/supervised learning for dialogue policies from communicator data. In *IJCAI workshop on knowledge and reasoning in practical dialogue systems*, pages 68–75. Citeseer.

Julian Hough and David Schlangen. 2017. It's not what you do, it's how you do it: Grounding uncertainty for a simple robot. In *Proceedings of the 2017 ACM/IEEE International Conference on Human-Robot Interaction*, pages 274–282. ACM.

Laura A Janda. 1988. The mapping of elements of cognitive space onto grammatical relations: An example from russian verbal prefixation. *Topics in cognitive linguistics*, 50:327–343.

Sahar Kazemzadeh, Vicente Ordonez, Mark Matten, and Tamara Berg. 2014. Referitgame: Referring to objects in photographs of natural scenes. In *Proceedings of the 2014 conference on empirical methods in natural language processing (EMNLP)*, pages 787–798.

Caroline Kery, Francis Ferraro, and Cynthia Matuszek. 2019. ¿ es un plátano? exploring the application of a physically grounded language acquisition system to spanish. In *Proceedings of the Combined Workshop on Spatial Language Understanding (SpLU) and Grounded Communication for Robotics (RoboNLP)*, pages 7–17.

Hyounghun Kim, Hao Tan, and Mohit Bansal. 2020. Modality-balanced models for visual dialogue.

Dimosthenis Kontogiorgos. 2017. Multimodal language grounding for improved human-robot collaboration: exploring spatial semantic representations in the shared space of attention. In *Proceedings of the 19th ACM International Conference on Multimodal Interaction*, pages 660–664. ACM.

Dimosthenis Kontogiorgos, Vanya Avramova, Simon Alexanderson, Patrik Jonell, Catharine Oertel, Jonas Beskow, Gabriel Skantze, and Joakim Gustafson. 2018. A multimodal corpus for mutual gaze and joint attention in multiparty situated interaction. In *International Conference on Language Resources and Evaluation (LREC 2018)*.

Staffan Larsson. 2018. Grounding as a side-effect of grounding. *Topics in Cognitive Science*, 10(2):389–408.

Séverin Lemaignan and Rachid Alami. 2013. talking to my robot: From knowledge grounding to dialogue processing. In *2013 8th ACM/IEEE International Conference on Human-Robot Interaction (HRI)*, pages 409–409. IEEE.

E. Levin, R. Pieraccini, and W. Eckert. 1998. Using markov decision process for learning dialogue strategies. In *Proceedings International Conference on Acoustics, Speech and Signal Processing (ICASSP)*.

Tomer Levinboim, Ashish Thapliyal, Piyush Sharma, and Radu Soricut. 2019. Quality estimation for image captions based on large-scale human evaluations. *arXiv preprint arXiv:1909.03396*.

Changsong Liu and Joyce Yue Chai. 2015. Learning to mediate perceptual differences in situated human-robot dialogue. In *Twenty-Ninth AAAI Conference on Artificial Intelligence*.

Ramesh Manuvinakurike, David DeVault, and Kallirroi Georgila. 2017. Using reinforcement learning to model incrementality in a fast-paced dialogue game. In *Proceedings of the 18th Annual SIGdial Meeting on Discourse and Dialogue*, pages 331–341.

Nikolaos Mavridis. 2015. A review of verbal and non-verbal human–robot interactive communication. *Robotics and Autonomous Systems*, 63:22–35.

Yukiko I Nakano, Gabe Reinstein, Tom Stocky, and Justine Cassell. 2003. Towards a model of face-to-face grounding. In *Proceedings of the 41st Annual Meeting on Association for Computational Linguistics-Volume 1*, pages 553–561. Association for Computational Linguistics.

Jekaterina Novikova, Oliver Lemon, and Verena Rieser. 2016. Crowd-sourcing nlg data: Pictures elicit better data. *arXiv preprint arXiv:1608.00339*.

Ian Perera, James Allen, Choh Man Teng, and Lucian Galescu. 2018. A situated dialogue system for learning structural concepts in blocks world. In *Proceedings of the 19th Annual SIGdial Meeting on Discourse and Dialogue*, pages 89–98.

Verena Rieser and Oliver Lemon. 2008. Learning effective multimodal dialogue strategies from Wizard-of-Oz data: Bootstrapping and evaluation. In *Proceedings of ACL-08: HLT*, pages 638–646, Columbus, Ohio. Association for Computational Linguistics.

Jonathan P Rowe, Eun Young Ha, and James C Lester. 2008. Archetype-driven character dialogue generation for interactive narrative. In *International Workshop on Intelligent Virtual Agents*. Springer.

Deb Roy. 2002. A trainable visually-grounded spoken language generation system. In *Proceedings of the international conference of spoken language processing*. Citeseer.

Ravi Shekhar, Aashish Venkatesh, Tim Baumgärtner, Elia Bruni, Barbara Plank, Raffaella Bernardi, and Raquel Fernández. 2018. Beyond task success: A closer look at jointly learning to see, ask, and guesswhat.

Candace L. Sidner, Christopher Lee, Cory D. Kidd, Neal Lesh, and Charles Rich. 2005. Explorations in engagement for humans and robots. *Artificial Intelligence*, 166(1):140 – 164.

Luc Steels. 2001. Language games for autonomous robots. *IEEE Intelligent systems*, 16(5):16–22.

Matthew Stone and Una Stojnić. 2015. Meaning and demonstration. *Review of Philosophy and Psychology*, 6:69–97.

Alane Suhr and Yoav Artzi. 2018. Situated mapping of sequential instructions to actions with single-step reward observation. In *Proceedings of the 56th Annual Meeting of the Association for Computational Linguistics (Volume 1: Long Papers)*, pages 2072–2082.

Alane Suhr, Stephanie Zhou, Ally Zhang, Iris Zhang, Huajun Bai, and Yoav Artzi. 2019. A corpus for reasoning about natural language grounded in photographs. In *Proceedings of the Annual Meeting of the Association for Computational Linguistics*.

Hao Tan and Mohit Bansal. 2018. Source-target inference models for spatial instruction understanding. In *Thirty-Second AAAI Conference on Artificial Intelligence*.

John Taylor et al. 1986. *Contrasting prepositional categories: English and Italian*. Linguistic Agency University of Duisburg.

Alberto Testoni, Ravi Shekhar, Raquel Fernández, and Raffaella Bernardi. 2019. The devil is in the details: A magnifying glass for the guesswhich visual dialogue game.

Jesse Thomason, Aishwarya Padmakumar, Jivko Sinapov, Nick Walker, Yuqian Jiang, Harel Yedidsion, Justin Hart, Peter Stone, and Raymond J Mooney. 2019. Improving grounded natural language understanding through human-robot dialog. *arXiv preprint arXiv:1903.00122*.

David R Traum. 1994. A computational theory of grounding in natural language conversation. Technical report, Rochester Univ NY Dept of Computer Science.

Marilyn A. Walker. 2000. An application of reinforcement learning to dialogue strategy selection in a spoken dialogue system for email. *J. Artif. Intell. Res. (JAIR)*, 12:387–416.

Joseph B Wiggins, Mayank Kulkarni, Wookhee Min, Kristy Elizabeth Boyer, Bradford Mott, Eric Wiebe, and James Lester. 2019. Take the initiative: Mixed initiative dialogue policies for pedagogical agents in game-based learning environments. In *International Conference on Artificial Intelligence in Education*. Springer.

Yanchao Yu, Arash Eshghi, and Oliver Lemon. 2016. Interactively learning visually grounded word meanings from a human tutor. In *Proceedings of the 5th Workshop on Vision and Language*.

Sina Zarrieß and David Schlangen. 2018. Being data-driven is not enough: Revisiting interactive instruction giving as a challenge for nlg. In *Proceedings of the Workshop on NLG for Human–Robot Interaction*, pages 27–31.

Hanwang Zhang, Yulei Niu, and Shih-Fu Chang. 2018. Grounding referring expressions in images by variational context. In *Proceedings of the IEEE Conference on Computer Vision and Pattern Recognition*, pages 4158–4166.

Reviewing Natural Language Processing Research

Kevin B. Cohen
Computational Bioscience Program
University of Colorado, USA
kevin.cohen@gmail.com

Karën Fort
Sorbonne Université, EA STIH, Paris
LORIA, Nancy
France
karen.fort@sorbonne-universite.fr

Margot Mieskes
University of Applied Sciences, Darmstadt
Germany
margot.mieskes@h-da.de

Aurélie Névéol
LIMSI, CNRS
Université Paris-Saclay
France
neveol@limsi.fr

1 Tutorial Content

This tutorial will cover the goals, processes, and evaluation of reviewing research in natural language processing. As has been pointed out for years by leading figures in our community (Webber, 2007), researchers in the ACL community face a heavy—and growing—reviewing burden. Initiatives to lower this burden have been discussed at the recent ACL general assembly in Florence (ACL 2019)[1]. Simultaneously, notable "false negatives"—rejection by our conferences of work that was later shown to be tremendously important after acceptance by *other* conferences (Church, 2005)—has raised awareness of the fact that our reviewing practices leave something to be desired... and we do not often talk about "false positives" with respect to conference papers, but conversations in the hallways at *ACL meetings suggest that we have a publication bias towards papers that report high performance, with perhaps not much else of interest in them (Manning, 2015).

It need not be this way. There is good reason to think that reviewing is a learnable (and teachable) skill (Basford, 1990; Paice, 2001; Benos et al., 2003; Koike et al., 2009; Shukla, 2010; Tandon, 2014; Spyns and Vidal, 2015; Stahel and Moore, 2016; Kohnen, 2017; McFadden et al., 2017; Hill, 2018). To address the issues raised above, we propose this tutorial on reviewing natural language processing research, focusing on conference submissions and various review forms used in the NLP community. The extended part also covers journal submissions.

As the demand for reviewing grows, so must the pool of reviewers. As the survey presented by Graham Neubig at the 2019 ACL showed, a considerable number of reviewers are junior researchers, who might lack the experience and expertise necessary for high-quality reviews. A tutorial on this topic might increase reviewers' confidence, as well as the quality of the reviews. Given the importance of conferences in NLP, the reviewing standards should be as high as with journals in other fields.

[1] http://www.livecongress.it/aol/indexSA.php?id=E2EAED7D&ticket=

2 Timetable

Table 1 shows an outline of the content discussed during the tutorial. Apart from a **general introduction** to the topic of peer reviewing and its role in the publishing circle, we will go into details on **reviewing for *ACL-venues**. All sections will include **exercises** and **practical** examples to get a better grasp for individual elements mentioned during the theoretical input. We will also take a look at **problems** with respect to peer reviewing and specific peer **reviewing models**, such as double-blind reviewing, which is the primary mode in *ACL-publication venues vs. single-blind and open reviewing. The **case study** will look at an actual example paper including reviews for that example.

3 Suggested Reading List

- John Bohannon. 2013. Who's afraid of peer review? *Science*, 342(6154):60–65
- Kenneth Church. 2005. Last words: Reviewing the reviewers. *Computational Linguistics*, 31(4):575–578
- Button K. S., Bal L., Clark A., and Shipley T. 2016. Preventing the ends from justifying the means: withholding results to address publication bias in peer-review. *BMC Psychol.*, 4(1)
- Leif Engqvist and Joachim Frommen. 2008. Double-blind peer review and gender publication bias. *Animal Behaviour*, 76:e1e2

Proceedings of the 58th Annual Meeting of the Association for Computational Linguistics, pages 16–18
July 5, 2020.
https://doi.org/10.18653/v1/P17

Section	Content
1	Role of peer review in scientific publishing
2	Approaches to reviewing and NLP-specific issues
3	Section-specific criteria (Materials & Methods, Results, etc.)
5	Ethics of reviewing
6	Case study: a paper to review

Table 1: Outline of the Tutorial.

- Michael J. Mahoney. 1977. Publication prejudices: An experimental study of confirmatory bias in the peer review system. *Cognitive Therapy and Research*, 1(2):161–175
- Mark Peplow. 2014. Peer review reviewed. *Nature*
- Mark Steedman. 2008. Last words: On becoming a discipline. *Computational Linguistics*, 34(1):137–144
- Bonnie Webber. 2007. Breaking news: Changing attitudes and practices. *Computational Linguistics*, 33(4):607–611
- Christine Wenners. 1997. Nepotism and sexism in peer-review. *Nature*, 387

4 Presenters (in alphabetical order)

Kevin Bretonnel Cohen has written, overseen, and received hundreds of reviews in his capacity as deputy editor-in-chief of a biomedical informatics journal, associate editor of five natural language processing or bioinformatics journals, special issue editor, workshop organizer, and author of 100+ publications in computational linguistics and natural language processing. His forthcoming book *Writing about data science research: With examples from machine and natural language processing* includes coverage of a number of aspects of the reviewing process. His current research focuses on issues of reproducibility.

Karën Fort is an associate professor at Sorbonne Université. Besides being a reviewer for most major NLP conferences, she has been editor in chief for a *Traitement automatique des langues* journal special issue on ethics and acted as Area Chair for ACL in 2017 and 2018 (as senior AC). Her main research interests are ethics, and the construction of language resources for natural language processing. She co-authored the report on the EMNLP reviewer survey (Névéol et al., 2017).

Margot Mieskes is a professor at the Darmstadt University of Applied Sciences and as such has a lot experience teaching, also in culturally diverse settings, which are prevalent in German Universities of Applied Sciences. Additionally, she has written and received a number of reviews in conferences as well as journals. She is a member of the ACL Professional Conduct Committee and an active member of the Widening NLP efforts. Her research interests are in summarization and summarization evaluation, replicability, repeatability and transparency of NLP experiments in general.

Aurélie Névéol is a permanent researcher at LIMSI CNRS and Université Paris Saclay. She has been involved in reviewing natural language processing papers at many stages of the reviewing process, including: reviewer, associate editor for three journals, area chair for *ACL and bioinformatics conferences, workshop organizer. Her research focuses on biomedical natural language processing as well as ethics issues in NLP research. She co-authored the report on EMNLP reviewer survey (Névéol et al., 2017).

References

P Basford. 1990. How to... review an article. *Nursing times*, 86(40):61–61.

Dale J Benos, Kevin L Kirk, and John E Hall. 2003. How to review a paper. *Advances in physiology education*, 27(2):47–52.

John Bohannon. 2013. Who's afraid of peer review? *Science*, 342(6154):60–65.

Kenneth Church. 2005. Last words: Reviewing the reviewers. *Computational Linguistics*, 31(4):575–578.

Leif Engqvist and Joachim Frommen. 2008. Double-blind peer review and gender publication bias. *Animal Behaviour*, 76:e1e2.

Michael D Hill. 2018. How to review a clinical research paper. *Stroke*, 49(5):e204–e206.

Thomas Kohnen. 2017. How to write a good peer review. *Journal of Cataract & Refractive Surgery*, 43(10):1243–1244.

Kaoru Koike, Luca Ansaloni, Fausto Catena, and Ernest E Moore. 2009. WJES: how to review a clinical paper. *World Journal of Emergency Surgery*, 4(1):8.

Michael J. Mahoney. 1977. Publication prejudices: An experimental study of confirmatory bias in the peer review system. *Cognitive Therapy and Research*, 1(2):161–175.

Christopher D Manning. 2015. Computational linguistics and deep learning. *Computational Linguistics*, 41(4):701–707.

David McFadden, Scott LeMaire, Michael Sarr, and Kevin Behrns. 2017. How to review a paper: Suggestions from the editors of surgery and the journal of surgical research. *Surgery*, 162(1):1–6.

Aurélie Névéol, Karën Fort, and Rebecca Hwa. 2017. Report on EMNLP Reviewer Survey. Technical report, Association for Computational Linguistics.

Elisabeth Paice. 2001. How to write a peer review. *Hospital Medicine*, 62(3):172–175.

Mark Peplow. 2014. Peer review reviewed. *Nature*.

Button K. S., Bal L., Clark A., and Shipley T. 2016. Preventing the ends from justifying the means: withholding results to address publication bias in peer-review. *BMC Psychol.*, 4(1).

Satish K Shukla. 2010. How to review an article. *Indian Journal of Surgery*, 72(2):93–96.

Peter Spyns and María-Esther Vidal. 2015. *Scientific Peer Reviewing: Practical Hints and Best Practices*. Springer.

Philip F Stahel and Ernest E Moore. 2016. How to review a surgical paper: a guide for junior referees. *BMC medicine*, 14(1):29.

Mark Steedman. 2008. Last words: On becoming a discipline. *Computational Linguistics*, 34(1):137–144.

Rajiv Tandon. 2014. How to review a scientific paper. *Asian journal of psychiatry*, 11:124–127.

Bonnie Webber. 2007. Breaking news: Changing attitudes and practices. *Computational Linguistics*, 33(4):607–611.

Christine Wenners. 1997. Nepotism and sexism in peer-review. *Nature*, 387.

Stylized Text Generation: Approaches and Applications

Lili Mou
University of Alberta; Amii
doublepower.mou@gmail.com

Olga Vechtomova
University of Waterloo
ovechtom@uwaterloo.ca

Type of Tutorial: Cutting-edge.

1 Tutorial Introduction

Text generation has played an important role in various applications of natural language processing (NLP), such as paraphrasing, summarization, and dialogue systems. With the development of modern deep learning techniques, text generation is usually accomplished by a neural decoder (e.g., a recurrent neural network or a Transformer), which generates a word at a time conditioned on previous generated words. The decoder can be further conditioned on some source information, such as a source language sentence in machine translation, or a previous utterance in dialogue systems.

In recent studies, researchers are paying increasing attention to modeling and manipulating the style of the generation text, which we call *stylized text generation* in this tutorial. The goal is to not only model the content of text (in traditional text generation), but also control some "style" of the text, for example, the persona of a speaker in a dialogue (Li et al., 2016), or the sentiment of product reviews (Hu et al., 2017).

Stylized text generation is related to various machine learning techniques, for example, embedding learning techniques to represent style (Fu et al., 2018), adversarial learning and reinforcement learning with cycle consistency to match "content" but to distinguish different styles (Hu et al., 2017; Xu et al., 2018; John et al., 2019); very recent work is even able to disentangle latent features in an unsupervised way (Xu et al., 2019).

In this tutorial, we will provide a comprehensive literature review on stylized text generation. We start from the definition of style and different settings of stylized text generation, illustrated with various applications.

In the second part, we will describe style-conditioned text generation. In this category, style serves as a certain type of source information, which the decoder is conditioned on. We describe three types of approaches: (1) embedding-based techniques that capture the style information by real-valued vectors, which can be used to condition a language model (Tikhonov and Yamshchikov, 2018) or concatenated with the input to a decoder (Li et al., 2016; Vechtomova et al., 2018) (2) approaches that encode both style and content in the latent space (Shi et al., 2019a; Yang et al., 2017; Li et al., 2020). We will discuss techniques that structure latent space to encode both style and content, and include Gaussian Mixture Model Variational Autoencoders (GMM-VAE) (Shi et al., 2019a; Wang et al., 2019a; Shi et al., 2019b), Conditional Variational Autoencoders (CVAE) (Yang et al., 2017), and Adversarially Regularized Autoencoders (ARAE) (Li et al., 2020). (3) approaches with multiple style-specific decoders (Syed et al., 2019; Chen et al., 2019). We highlight several applications including persona-based dialogue generation (Li et al., 2016) and creative writing (Yang et al., 2017; Tikhonov and Yamshchikov, 2018; Vechtomova et al., 2018).

Next, we will introduce evaluation methods for style-conditioned text generation. We will present the current practice in the literature, involving both human evaluation and automatic metrics. A few important evaluation aspects include the success of being in the target style, the preservation of content information, as well as language fluency in general.

In the third part, we will focus on style-transfer text generation. Given an input sentence of a certain style, the goal of style transfer is to synthesize a new sentence that has the same content but with different styles. Particularly, style-transfer text generation can be categorized into three settings: (1) Parallel-supervised style transfer, where a par-

Proceedings of the 58th Annual Meeting of the Association for Computational Linguistics, pages 19–22
July 5, 2020. ©2020 Association for Computational Linguistics
https://doi.org/10.18653/v1/P17

allel corpus is available (Xu et al., 2012; Rao and Tetreault, 2018). This is similar to machine translation, but semi-supervised learning is adopted to address small-data training (Wang et al., 2019b). (2) Non-parallel style transfer, where each sentence is annotated by a style label (e.g., positive or negative sentiment). This setting is the most explored setting in previous style transfer literature. We will discuss classification losses to distinguish different styles (John et al., 2019), and adversarial losses/cycle consistency to match content information (Shen et al., 2017). We will also present an editing-based approach that edits style-specific words and phrases into the desired style (Li et al., 2018). (3) Unsupervised style transfer, where the entire corpus is unlabeled (no parallel pairs or style labels). In recent studies, researchers have applied auxiliary losses (such as orthogonality penalty) to detect the most prevalent variation of text in a corpus, and are sometimes able to accomplish style transfer in a purely unsupervised fashion. Since unsupervised style transfer is new to NLP and less explored, we will also introduce several studies in the computer vision domain, bringing future opportunities to text generation in this setting (Gatys et al., 2016; Chen et al., 2016).

Next, we will discuss style adversarial text generation (Zhang et al., 2019). The setting of adversarial attacks is similar to style transfer in that it aims to change the style classifier's prediction. However, the synthesized sentence in this setting should in fact keep the actual style as humans perceive, but "fool" the style classifier. Thus, it is known as the *adversarial attack*. We will discuss style adversarial generation in the character level, the word level, as well as the sentence level. Techniques include discrete word manipulation and continuous latent space manipulation.

Finally, we will conclude our tutorial by presenting the challenges of stylized text generation and discussing future directions, such as small-data training, non-categorical style modeling, and a generalized scope of style transfer (e.g., controlling the syntax as a style (Bao et al., 2019)).

By the end of the tutorial, the audience will have a systematic view of different settings of stylized text generation, understand common techniques to model and manipulate the style of text, and be able to apply existing approaches to new scenarios that require stylized text generation. Our tutorial also investigates stylized generative models in non-NLP domains, and thus would inspire future NLP studies in this direction.

2 Tutorial Outline

PART I: Introduction (20 min)

- Definition of style
- Settings and Problem formulations
- Examples of style (e.g., sentiment, artistic style, grammatical style)

PART II: Style-Conditioned Text Generation (50 min)

- Techniques
  - Encoding style in embeddings: sequence-to-sequence models with style embeddings, style conditioned language models, Variational Autoencoder (VAE) with style embeddings;
  - Encoding style and content in latent space: Conditional Variational Autoencoder (CVAE) Gaussian Mixture Variational Autoencoder (GMM-VAE), Adversarially Regularized Autoencoder (ARAE).
  - Models with multiple style-specific decoders
- Applications
  - Creative text generation (e.g., poetry composition)
  - Persona and emotion conditioned dialogue models
  - Stylized image caption generation
- Evaluation measures
  - Stylistic adherence
  - Content preservation
  - Language fluency
  - Novelty and diversity

PART III: Style-Transfer Text Generation (60 min)

- Parallel supervised style transfer
  - Sequence-to-sequence learning
  - Semi-supervised training with limited parallel data

– Applications: Shakespearean–modern English transfer, formality style transfer

- Non-parallel supervised style transfer
  – Auxiliary classification for style modeling
  – Adversarial learning for matching content
  – Cycle consistency for content matching
  – Edit-based style transfer
  – Applications: Sentiment, genre and grammatical style transfer

- Unsupervised style transfer
  – Approaches: Mutual information penalties and correlation penalties for automatic style detection
  – A brief introduction of unsupervised style transfer in image domain (e.g., color, shape, angle)

PART IV: Style-Advsersarial Text Generation (30 minutes)

- Style adversarial vs. style transfer
- Approaches
  – Character-level attack
  – Word-level attack
  – Sentence-level attack

PART IV: Conclusion, Future Work, and Q&A (20 min)

- Challenges: non-categorical style, small-data training
- A broader view of "style": text summarization/simplification as style transfer, syntax-semantic disentanglement

3 Instructors

Lili Mou
doublepower.mou@gmail.com
https://lili-mou.github.io

Dr. Lili Mou is an Assistant Professor at the Department of Computing Science, University of Alberta. He is also an Amii Fellow and a Canadian CIFAR AI Chair. Lili received his BS and PhD degrees in 2012 and 2017, respectively, from School of EECS, Peking University. After that, he worked as a postdoctoral fellow at the University of Waterloo and a research scientist at Adeptmind (a startup in Toronto, Canada). His research interests include deep learning applied to natural language processing as well as programming language processing. Recently, he has been focusing more on text generation, from both continuous latent space and discrete word space. He has more than 30 papers published at top-tier conferences and journals, including AAAI, ACL, CIKM, COLING, EMNLP, ICASSP, ICLR, ICML, IJCAI, INTERSPEECH, NAACL-HLT, and TACL. He presented a tutorial "*Discreteness in Neural Natural Language Processing*" at EMNLP-IJCNLP'19.

Olga Vechtomova
ovechtomova@uwaterloo.ca
https://ov-research.uwaterloo.ca

Dr. Olga Vechtomova is an Associate Professor in the Department of Management Sciences, Faculty of Engineering, cross-appointed in the School of Computer Science at the University of Waterloo. Olga leads the Natural Language Processing Lab, affiliated with the Waterloo.AI Institute. Her research has been supported by a number of industry and government grants, including Amazon Research Award and Natural Sciences and Engineering Research Council (NSERC). The research in her Lab is mainly focused on designing deep neural networks for natural language generation tasks. Her current and recent projects include controlled text generation, text style transfer, and designing text generative models for creative applications. She has over 50 publications in NLP and Information Retrieval conferences and journals, including NAACL-HLT, COLING, ACL, ACM SIGIR, and CIKM. She and her colleagues recently received the ACM SIGIR 2019 Test of Time Award.

Acknowledgments

We acknowledge the support of the Natural Sciences and Engineering Research Council of Canada (NSERC), under grant Nos. RGPIN-2019-04897 and RGPIN-2020-04465. Lili Mou is also supported by AltaML, the Amii Fellow Program, and the Canadian CIFAR AI Chair Program.

References

Yu Bao, Hao Zhou, Shujian Huang, Lei Li, Lili Mou, Olga Vechtomova, Xin-yu Dai, and Jiajun Chen. 2019. Generating sentences from disentangled syntactic and semantic spaces. In *ACL*, pages 6008–6019.

Cheng-Kuan Chen, Zhufeng Pan, Ming-Yu Liu, and Min Sun. 2019. Unsupervised stylish image description generation via domain layer norm. In *Proceedings of the AAAI Conference on Artificial Intelligence*, volume 33, pages 8151–8158.

Xi Chen, Yan Duan, Rein Houthooft, John Schulman, Ilya Sutskever, and Pieter Abbeel. 2016. InfoGAN: Interpretable representation learning by information maximizing generative adversarial nets. In *NIPS*, pages 2172–2180.

Zhenxin Fu, Xiaoye Tan, Nanyun Peng, Dongyan Zhao, and Rui Yan. 2018. Style transfer in text: Exploration and evaluation. In *AAAI*, pages 663–670.

Leon A Gatys, Alexander S Ecker, and Matthias Bethge. 2016. Image style transfer using convolutional neural networks. In *CVPR*, pages 2414–2423.

Zhiting Hu, Zichao Yang, Xiaodan Liang, Ruslan Salakhutdinov, and Eric P Xing. 2017. Toward controlled generation of text. In *ICML*, pages 1587–1596.

Vineet John, Lili Mou, Hareesh Bahuleyan, and Olga Vechtomova. 2019. Disentangled representation learning for non-parallel text style transfer. In *ACL*, pages 424–434.

Jiwei Li, Michel Galley, Chris Brockett, Georgios Spithourakis, Jianfeng Gao, and Bill Dolan. 2016. A persona-based neural conversation model. In *ACL*, pages 994–1003.

Juncen Li, Robin Jia, He He, and Percy Liang. 2018. Delete, retrieve, generate: a simple approach to sentiment and style transfer. In *NAACL-HLT*, pages 1865–1874.

Yuan Li, Chunyuan Li, Yizhe Zhang, Xiujun Li, Guoqing Zheng, Lawrence Carin, and Jianfeng Gao. 2020. Complementary auxiliary classifiers for label-conditional text generation. In *AAAI*.

Sudha Rao and Joel Tetreault. 2018. Dear sir or madam, may I introduce the GYAFC dataset: Corpus, benchmarks and metrics for formality style transfer. In *NAACL-HLT*, pages 129–140.

Tianxiao Shen, Tao Lei, Regina Barzilay, and Tommi Jaakkola. 2017. Style transfer from non-parallel text by cross-alignment. In *NIPS*, pages 6830–6841.

Wenxian Shi, Hao Zhou, Ning Miao, Shenjian Zhao, and Lei Li. 2019a. Fixing Gaussian mixture VAEs for interpretable text generation. *arXiv preprint arXiv:1906.06719*.

Wenxian Shi, Hao Zhou, Ning Miao, Shenjian Zhao, and Lei Li. 2019b. Fixing Gaussian mixture VAEs for interpretable text generation. *arXiv preprint arXiv:1906.06719*.

Bakhtiyar Syed, Gaurav Verma, Balaji Vasan Srinivasan, Vasudeva Varma, et al. 2019. Adapting language models for non-parallel author-stylized rewriting. *arXiv preprint arXiv:1909.09962*.

Alexey Tikhonov and Ivan P Yamshchikov. 2018. Guess who? multilingual approach for the automated generation of author-stylized poetry. In *IEEE Spoken Language Technology Workshop*, pages 787–794.

Olga Vechtomova, Hareesh Bahuleyan, Amirpasha Ghabussi, and Vineet John. 2018. Generating lyrics with variational autoencoder and multi-modal artist embeddings. *arXiv preprint arXiv:1812.08318*.

Wenlin Wang, Zhe Gan, Hongteng Xu, Ruiyi Zhang, Guoyin Wang, Dinghan Shen, Changyou Chen, and Lawrence Carin. 2019a. Topic-guided variational autoencoders for text generation. *arXiv preprint arXiv:1903.07137*.

Yunli Wang, Yu Wu, Lili Mou, Zhoujun Li, and Wenhan Chao. 2019b. Harnessing pre-trained neural networks with rules for formality style transfer. In *EMNLP-IJCNLP*.

Jingjing Xu, Xu Sun, Qi Zeng, Xiaodong Zhang, Xuancheng Ren, Houfeng Wang, and Wenjie Li. 2018. Unpaired sentiment-to-sentiment translation: A cycled reinforcement learning approach. In *ACL*, pages 979–988.

Peng Xu, Yanshuai Cao, and Jackie Chi Kit Cheung. 2019. Unsupervised controllable text generation with global variation discovery and disentanglement. *arXiv preprint arXiv:1905.11975*.

Wei Xu, Alan Ritter, Bill Dolan, Ralph Grishman, and Colin Cherry. 2012. Paraphrasing for style. In *COLING*, pages 2899–2914.

Xiaopeng Yang, Xiaowen Lin, Shunda Suo, and Ming Li. 2017. Generating thematic chinese poetry using conditional variational autoencoders with hybrid decoders. *arXiv preprint arXiv:1711.07632*.

Huangzhao Zhang, Hao Zhou, Ning Miao, and Lei Li. 2019. Generating fluent adversarial examples for natural languages. In *ACL*, pages 5564–5569, Florence, Italy.

Multi-modal Information Extraction from Text, Semi-structured, and Tabular Data on the Web

Xin Luna Dong
Amazon
lunadong@amazon.com

Hannaneh Hajishirzi
University of Washington
Allen Institute for AI
hannaneh@washington.edu

Colin Lockard
University of Washington
lockardc@cs.washington.edu

Prashant Shiralkar
Amazon
shiralp@amazon.com

Abstract

How do we surface the large amount of information present in HTML documents on the Web, from news articles to Rotten Tomatoes pages to tables of sports scores? Such information can enable a variety of applications including knowledge base construction, question answering, recommendation, and more. In this tutorial, we present approaches for information extraction (IE) from Web data that can be differentiated along two key dimensions: 1) the diversity in data modality that is leveraged, e.g. text, visual, XML/HTML, and 2) the thrust to develop scalable approaches with zero to limited human supervision.

1 Description

Motivation: The World Wide Web contains vast quantities of textual information in several forms: unstructured text, template-based semi-structured webpages (which present data in key-value pairs and lists), and tables. Methods for extracting information from these sources and converting it to a structured form have been a target of research from the natural language processing (NLP), data mining, and database communities. While these researchers have largely separated extraction from web data into different problems based on the modality of the data, they have faced similar problems such as learning with limited labeled data, defining (or avoiding defining) ontologies, making use of prior knowledge, and scaling solutions to deal with the size of the Web.

In this tutorial we take a holistic view toward information extraction, exploring the commonalities in the challenges and solutions developed to address these different forms of text. We will explore the approaches targeted at unstructured text that largely rely on learning syntactic or semantic textual patterns, approaches targeted at semi-structured documents that learn to identify structural patterns in the template, and approaches targeting web tables which rely heavily on entity linking and type information.

While these different data modalities have largely been considered separately in the past, recent research has started taking a more inclusive approach toward textual extraction, in which the multiple signals offered by textual, layout, and visual clues are combined into a single extraction model made possible by new deep learning approaches. At the same time, trends within purely textual extraction have shifted toward full-document understanding rather than considering sentences as independent units. With this in mind, it is worth considering the information extraction problem as a whole to motivate solutions that harness textual semantics along with visual and semi-structured layout information. We will discuss these approaches and suggest avenues for future work.

Tutorial Content: We will start by defining unstructured, semi-structured, and tabular text, and discussing the challenges and opportunities that differentiate these data sources, as well as those they have in common. We will then provide introductions to the basic models and learning algorithms used in extraction from unstructured, semi-structured, and tabular text. We will pay special attention to methods that enable extraction to be expanded to the scope of entity and relation types found on the web, such as the distant supervision and data programming paradigms of creating training data, and schema-less "OpenIE" extraction. After introducing the separate approaches targeting these data modalities, we will then explore research that combines signals from textual, visual, and layout information to consider all aspects of a document.

Throughout the tutorial, we will bring together lessons learned from the different communities involved in information extraction research and will

Proceedings of the 58th Annual Meeting of the Association for Computational Linguistics, pages 23–26
July 5, 2020.
https://doi.org/10.18653/v1/P17

provide insights from industry experiences building a production knowledge graph leveraging both unstructured and semi-structured text. Section 3 contains a full outline of planned content.

Tutorial slides are available at `https://sites.google.com/view/acl-2020-multi-modal-ie`

Relevance to ACL: Information Extraction is a core task in natural language processing, with the web serving as a rich source of information for constructing knowledge bases (KBs). A 2018 NAACL tutorial, "Scalable Construction and Reasoning of Massive Knowlege Bases" (Ren et al., 2018), provided an overview of recent IE and KB research. However, like most NLP research, that tutorial focused on methods that treat text as a simple string of natural language sentences in a `txt` file, while many real-world documents convey information via visual and layout relationships. A separate line of information extraction work has focused on learning to extract from these template-based documents. As interest in multi-modal NLP techniques has grown in recent years, we think the community will be interested in a tutorial that compares and contrasts these approaches and examines recent research that brings together textual, visual, and layout features of documents.

2 Type of the tutorial:

The tutorial will cover **cutting-edge** work in both unstructured and semi-structured information extraction, including visual and GCN-based approaches. However, our coverage of semi-structured and tabular IE will cover **introductory** material since it is likely new to much of the NLP community.

3 Outline

1. **(30 mins) Introduction and Applications**
    - Knowledge Base Population
        - Intro to knowledge graphs
        - Applications
        - Industry examples
        - Importance of the long tail
    - Unstructured, Semi-structured, and Tabular text
        - Unstructured Text
        - HTML and DOM trees
        - Webtables
        - Template learning vs. generalization
    - Schema-aligned extraction vs. OpenIE
    - Common challenges, opportunities, and key intuitions
2. **(45 mins) IE from unstructured text:**
    - Tasks
        - Named Entity Recognition
        - Co-reference Resolution
        - Relation Extraction
        - Event Extraction
    - Featurization and Modeling
        - OpenTag (Zheng et al., 2018)
        - DyGIE (Luan et al., 2019)
    - Limited Training Data
        - Distant Supervision (Mintz et al., 2009)
        - Data Programming (Ratner et al., 2017)
    - OpenIE
3. **(45 mins) IE from semi-structured documents**
    - Supervised Wrapper Induction
        - Vertex (Gulhane et al., 2011)
    - Distantly Supervised approaches
        - LODIE (Ciravegna et al., 2012)
        - DIADEM (Furche et al., 2012)
        - Ceres (Lockard et al., 2018)
    - OpenIE / Schema-less approaches
        - WEIR (Bronzi et al., 2013)
        - OpenCeres (Lockard et al., 2019)
4. **(15 mins) IE from tables**
    - WebTables (Cafarella et al., 2018)
    - Subject detection (Venetis et al., 2011)
    - Joint approaches (LimayeGirija et al., 2010)
5. **(30 mins) Multi-modal extraction**
    - Benefits of multi-modal extraction
        - Connecting tables and text (Ibrahim et al., 2019)
        - Visual signals for keyphrase extraction (Xiong et al., 2019)
        - Documents as images (Katti et al., 2018)
        - GCN-based encoders (Qian et al., 2019; Liu et al., 2019)
    - Multi-modal signals for creating training data (Wu et al., 2018)

- Multi-modal OpenIE

6. **(15 mins) Conclusion and Open Directions**

4 Prerequisites

The tutorial should be accessible to anyone with a background in natural language processing. It would be helpful to have a basic understanding of classification algorithms, preferably with some knowledge of neural network approaches, as well as unsupervised clustering algorithms.

5 Reading list

- "Web-Scale Information Extraction With Vertex", Gulhane et al. (2011)
- "Ten Years of WebTables", Cafarella et al. (2018)
- "Fonduer: Knowledge Base Construction from Richly Formatted Data", Wu et al. (2018)
- "Document-level N-ary Relation Extraction with Multi-Scale Representation Learning", Jia et al. (2019)
- "Extraction and Integration of Partially Overlapping Web Sources" Bronzi et al. (2013)
- "Knowledge Vault: A Web-Scale Approach to Probabilistic Knowledge Fusion", Dong et al. (2014)
- "A General Framework for Information Extraction Using Dynamic Span Graphs", Luan et al. (2019)
- "OpenCeres: When Open Information Extraction Meets the Semi-Structured Web", Lockard et al. (2019)
- "GraphIE: A Graph-Based Framework for Information Extraction", Qian et al. (2019)

6 Presenters

In alphabetical order,

Xin Luna Dong is a Principal Scientist at Amazon, leading the efforts of constructing Amazon Product Knowledge Graph. She was one of the major contributors to the Google Knowledge Vault project, and has led the Knowledge-based Trust project, which is called the "Google Truth Machine" by the Washington Post. She co-authored the book "Big Data Integration", was awarded ACM Distinguished Member, VLDB Early Career Research Contribution Award for "advancing the state of the art of knowledge fusion", and Best Demo award in Sigmod 2005. She serves on the VLDB endowment and PVLDB advisory committee, and was a PC co-chair for VLDB 2021, ICDE Industry 2019, VLDB Tutorial 2019, Sigmod 2018 and WAIM 2015. She has given multiple tutorials on data integration, graph mining, and knowledge management.
Email: lunadong@amazon.com
Homepage: http://lunadong.com/.

Hannaneh Hajishirzi is an Assistant Professor at the Paul G. Allen School of Computer Science & Engineering at the University of Washington. She works on NLP, AI, and machine learning, particularly designing algorithms for semantic understanding, reasoning, question answering, and information extraction from multimodal data. She has earned numerous awards for her research, including an Allen Distinguished Investigator Award, a Google Faculty Research Award, a Bloomberg Data Science Award, an Amazon Research Award, and a SIGDIAL Best Paper Award.
Email: hannaneh@washington.edu
Homepage:
https://homes.cs.washington.edu/ hannaneh/

Colin Lockard is a PhD student at the Paul G. Allen School of Computer Science & Engineering at the University of Washington, where he has published papers on knowledge extraction from both unstructured and semi-structured text.
Email: lockardc@cs.washington.edu
Homepage:
https://homes.cs.washington.edu/ lockardc/

Prashant Shiralkar is an Applied Scientist in the Product Graph team at Amazon. He currently works on knowledge extraction from semi-structured data. Previously, he received a Ph.D. from Indiana University Bloomington where his dissertation work focused on devising computational approaches for fact checking by mining knowledge graphs. His research interests include machine learning, data mining, information extraction and NLP, and Semantic Web technologies.
Email: shiralp@amazon.com
Homepage:
https://sites.google.com/site/shiralkarprashant/

References

Mirko Bronzi, Valter Crescenzi, Paolo Merialdo, and Paolo Papotti. 2013. Extraction and integration of partially overlapping web sources. *VLDB*, 6(10):805–816.

Michael Cafarella, Alon Halevy, Hongrae Lee, Jayant Madhavan, Cong Yu, Daisy Zhe Wang, and Eugene Wu. 2018. Ten years of webtables. *VLDB*, 11(12):2140–2149.

Fabio Ciravegna, Anna Lisa Gentile, and Ziqi Zhang. 2012. LODIE: Linked open data for web-scale information extraction. *SWAIE*, 925:11–22.

Xin Luna Dong, Evgeniy Gabrilovich, Geremy Heitz, Wilko Horn, Kevin Murphy, Shaohua Sun, and Wei Zhang. 2014. From data fusion to knowledge fusion. *VLDB*, 7(10):881–892.

Tim Furche, Georg Gottlob, Giovanni Grasso, Omer Gunes, Xiaoanan Guo, Andrey Kravchenko, Giorgio Orsi, Christian Schallhart, Andrew Sellers, and Cheng Wang. 2012. Diadem: domain-centric, intelligent, automated data extraction methodology. In *WWW*, pages 267–270. ACM.

Pankaj Gulhane, Amit Madaan, Rupesh Mehta, Jeyashankher Ramamirtham, Rajeev Rastogi, Sandeep Satpal, Srinivasan H Sengamedu, Ashwin Tengli, and Charu Tiwari. 2011. Web-scale information extraction with vertex. In *ICDE*, pages 1209–1220. IEEE.

Yusra Ibrahim, Mirek Riedewald, Gerhard Weikum, and Demetrios Zeinalipour-Yazti. 2019. Bridging quantities in tables and text. *ICDE*, pages 1010–1021.

Robin Jia, Cliff Wong, and Hoifung Poon. 2019. Document-level n-ary relation extraction with multiscale representation learning. In *NAACL-HLT*, pages 3693–3704, Minneapolis, Minnesota. Association for Computational Linguistics.

Anoop Raveendra Katti, Christian Reisswig, Cordula Guder, Sebastian Brarda, Steffen Bickel, Johannes Höhne, and Jean Baptiste Faddoul. 2018. Chargrid: Towards understanding 2d documents. *EMNLP*.

LimayeGirija, SarawagiSunita, and ChakrabartiSoumen. 2010. Annotating and searching web tables using entities, types and relationships. In *VLDB 2010*.

Xiaojing Liu, Feiyu Gao, Qiong Zhang, and Huasha Zhao. 2019. Graph convolution for multimodal information extraction from visually rich documents. In *NAACL-HLT*.

Colin Lockard, Xin Luna Dong, Arash Einolghozati, and Prashant Shiralkar. 2018. Ceres: distantly supervised relation extraction from the semi-structured web. *VLDB*, 11(10):1084–1096.

Colin Lockard, Prashant Shiralkar, and Xin Luna Dong. 2019. OpenCeres: When open information extraction meets the semi-structured web. In *NAACL-HLT*, pages 3047–3056.

Yi Luan, Dave Wadden, Luheng He, Amy Shah, Mari Ostendorf, and Hannaneh Hajishirzi. 2019. A general framework for information extraction using dynamic span graphs. In *NAACL-HLT*.

Mike Mintz, Steven Bills, Rion Snow, and Daniel Jurafsky. 2009. Distant supervision for relation extraction without labeled data. In *ACL/IJCNLP*.

Yujie Qian, Enrico Santus, Zhijing Jin, Jiang Guo, and Regina Barzilay. 2019. Graphie: A graph-based framework for information extraction. In *NAACL-HLT*.

Alexander J. Ratner, Stephen H. Bach, Henry R. Ehrenberg, and Christopher Ré. 2017. Snorkel: Fast training set generation for information extraction. In *SIGMOD*.

Xiang Ren, Nanyun Peng, and William Yang Wang. 2018. Scalable construction and reasoning of massive knowledge bases. In *NAACL-HLT, Tutorial Abstracts*, pages 10–16.

Petros Venetis, Alon Y. Halevy, Jayant Madhavan, Marius Pasca, Warren Shen, Fei Wu, Gengxin Miao, and Chung Wu. 2011. Recovering semantics of tables on the web. *PVLDB*, 4:528–538.

Sen Wu, Luke Hsiao, Xiao Cheng, Braden Hancock, Theodoros Rekatsinas, Philip Levis, and Christopher Ré. 2018. Fonduer: Knowledge base construction from richly formatted data. *SIGMOD*, 2018:1301–1316.

Lee Xiong, Chuan Hu, Chenyan Xiong, Daniel Fernando Campos, and Arnold Overwijk. 2019. Open domain web keyphrase extraction beyond language modeling. In *EMNLP/IJCNLP*.

Guineng Zheng, Subhabrata Mukherjee, Xin Luna Dong, and Feifei Li. 2018. OpenTag: Open attribute value extraction from product profiles. In *KDD*, pages 1049–1058. ACM.

Introductory Tutorial: Commonsense Reasoning for Natural Language Processing

Maarten Sap [1] **Vered Shwartz** [1,2] **Antoine Bosselut** [1,2] **Yejin Choi** [1,2] **Dan Roth** [3]
[1] Paul G. Allen School of Computer Science & Engineering, Seattle, WA, USA
[2] Allen Institute for Artificial Intelligence, Seattle, WA, USA
[3] Department of Computer and Information Science, University of Pennsylvania
{msap, vereds, antoineb, yejin} @cs.washington.edu, danroth@seas.upenn.edu

1 Introduction

Commonsense knowledge, such as knowing that "bumping into people annoys them" or "rain makes the road slippery", helps humans navigate everyday situations seamlessly (Apperly, 2010). Yet, endowing machines with such human-like commonsense reasoning capabilities has remained an elusive goal of artificial intelligence research for decades (Gunning, 2018).

Commonsense knowledge and reasoning have received renewed attention from the natural language processing (NLP) community in recent years, yielding multiple exploratory research directions into automated commonsense understanding. Recent efforts to acquire and represent common knowledge resulted in large knowledge graphs, acquired through extractive methods (Speer et al., 2017) or crowdsourcing (Sap et al., 2019a). Simultaneously, a large body of work in integrating reasoning capabilities into downstream tasks has emerged, allowing the development of smarter dialogue (Zhou et al., 2018) and question answering agents (Xiong et al., 2019).

Recent advances in large pretrained language models (e.g., Devlin et al., 2019; Liu et al., 2019b), however, have pushed machines closer to human-like understanding capabilities, calling into question whether machines should directly model commonsense through symbolic integrations. But despite these impressive performance improvements in a variety of NLP tasks, it remains unclear whether these models are performing complex reasoning, or if they are merely learning complex surface correlation patterns (Davis and Marcus, 2015; Marcus, 2018). This difficulty in measuring the progress in commonsense reasoning using downstream tasks has yielded increased efforts at developing robust benchmarks for directly measuring commonsense capabilities in multiple settings, such as social interactions (Sap et al., 2019b; Rashkin et al., 2018a) and physical situations (Zellers et al., 2019; Talmor et al., 2019).

We hope that in the future, machines develop the kind of intelligence required to, for example, properly assist humans in everyday situations (e.g., a chatbot that anticipates the needs of an elderly person; Pollack, 2005). Current methods, however, are still not powerful or robust enough to be deployed in open-domain production settings, despite the clear improvements provided by large-scale pretrained language models. This shortcoming is partially due to inadequacy in acquiring, understanding and reasoning about commonsense knowledge, topics which remain understudied by the larger NLP, AI, and Vision communities relative to its importance in building AI agents. We organize this tutorial to provide researchers with information about the critical foundations and recent advances in commonsense, in the hopes of casting a brighter light on this promising area of future research.

In our tutorial, we will (1) outline the various types of commonsense (e.g., physical, social), and (2) discuss techniques to gather and represent commonsense knowledge, while highlighting the challenges specific to this type of knowledge (e.g., reporting bias). We will also (3) discuss the types of commonsense knowledge captured by modern NLP systems (e.g., large pretrained language models), (4) review ways to incorporate commonsense knowledge into downstream task models, and (5) present various benchmarks used to measure systems' commonsense reasoning abilities.

2 Description

What is commonsense? The tutorial will start with a brief overview of what commonsense is, how it is defined in the literature, and how hu-

Proceedings of the 58th Annual Meeting of the Association for Computational Linguistics, pages 27–33
July 5, 2020. ©2020 Association for Computational Linguistics
https://doi.org/10.18653/v1/P17

mans acquire it (Moore, 2013; Baron-Cohen et al., 1985). We will discuss notions of social commonsense (Burke, 1969; Goldman, 2015) and physical commonsense (Hayes, 1978; McRae et al., 2005). We will cover the differences between taxonomic and inferential knowledge (Davis and Marcus, 2015; Pearl and Mackenzie, 2018), and differentiate commonsense knowledge from related concepts (e.g., script learning; Schank and Abelson, 1975; Chambers and Jurafsky, 2008).

How to represent commonsense? We will review existing methods for representing commonsense, most of which focus solely on English. At first, symbolic logic approaches were the main representation type (Forbus, 1989; Lenat, 1995). While still in use today (Davis, 2017; Gordon and Hobbs, 2017), computational advances have allowed for more data-driven knowledge collection and representation (e.g., automatic extraction; Etzioni et al., 2008; Zhang et al., 2016; Elazar et al., 2019). We will cover recent approaches that use natural language to represent commonsense (Speer et al., 2017; Sap et al., 2019a), and while noting the challenges that come with using data-driven methods (Gordon and Van Durme, 2013; Jastrzebski et al., 2018).

What do machines know? Pretrained language models (LMs) have recently been described as "rediscovering the NLP pipeline" (Tenney et al., 2019a), i.e. replacing previous dedicated components of the traditional NLP pipeline, starting from low- and mid-level syntactic and semantic tasks (POS tagging, parsing, verb agreement, e.g., Peters et al., 2018; Jawahar et al., 2019; Shwartz and Dagan, 2019, *inter alia*), to high-level semantic tasks such as named entity recognition, coreference resolution and semantic role labeling (Tenney et al., 2019b; Liu et al., 2019a). We will discuss recent investigations into pretrained LMs' ability to capture world knowledge (Petroni et al., 2019; Logan et al., 2019) and learn or reason about commonsense (Feldman et al., 2019).

How to incorporate commonsense knowledge into downstream models? Given that large number of NLP applications are designed to require commonsense reasoning, we will review efforts to integrate such knowledge into NLP tasks. Various works have looked at directly encoding commonsense knowledge from structured KBs as additional inputs to a neural network in generation (Guan et al., 2018), dialogue (Zhou et al., 2018), QA (Mihaylov and Frank, 2018; Bauer et al., 2018; Lin et al., 2019; Weissenborn et al., 2017; Musa et al., 2019), and classification (Chen et al., 2018; Paul and Frank, 2019; Wang et al., 2018) tasks. For applications without available structured knowledge bases, researchers have relied on commonsense aggregated from corpus statistics pulled from unstructured text (Tandon et al., 2018; Lin et al., 2017; Li et al., 2018; Banerjee et al., 2019). More recently, rather than providing relevant commonsense as an additional input to neural networks, researchers have looked into indirectly encoding commonsense knowledge into the parameters of neural networks through pretraining on commonsense knowledge bases (Zhong et al., 2018) or explanations (Rajani et al., 2019), or by using multi-task objectives with commonsense relation prediction (Xia et al., 2019).

How to measure machines' ability of commonsense reasoning? We will explain that, despite their design, many natural language understanding (NLU) tasks hardly require machines to reason about commonsense (Lo Bue and Yates, 2011; Schwartz et al., 2017). This prompted efforts in creating benchmarks carefully designed to be impossible to solve without commonsense knowledge (Roemmele et al., 2011; Levesque, 2011).

In response, recent work has focused on using crowdsourcing and automatic filtering to design large-scale benchmarks while maintaining negative examples that are adversarial to machines (Zellers et al., 2018). We will review recent benchmarks that have emerged to assess whether machines have acquired physical (e.g., Talmor et al., 2019; Zellers et al., 2019), social (e.g., Sap et al., 2019b), or temporal commonsense reasoning capabilities (e.g., Zhou et al., 2019), as well as benchmarks that combine commonsense abilities with other tasks (e.g., reading comprehension; Ostermann et al., 2018; Zhang et al., 2018; Huang et al., 2019).

3 Outline

3.1 Schedule

Talk 1 (15 min.) will introduce and motivate this tutorial and discuss long term vision for NLP commonsense research.

Talk 2 (20 min.) will focus on the question "Do pre-trained language models capture commonsense knowledge?" and review recent work that studies what such models already capture due to their pre-training, what they can be fine-tuned to capture, and what types of knowledge are not captured.

Talk 3 (20 min.) will discuss ways of defining and representing commonsense, covering established symbolic methods and recent efforts for natural language representations.

Talk 4 (20 min.) will discuss neural and symbolic models of commonsense reasoning, focusing on models based on external knowledge integration for downstream tasks.

If time permits, we will end the first half with an interactive session and a preview to the second half.

Break (30 min.)

Talk 5 (20 min.) will continue the discussion on neural and symbolic models of commonsense knowledge representation, focusing on COMET (Bosselut et al., 2019), a language model trained on commonsense knowledge graphs. We will present its utility in a zero-shot model for a downstream commonsense question answering task.

Talk 6 (25 min.) will focus on temporal commonsense: how to represent it, how to incorporate it into downstream models, and how to test it.

Talk 7 (20 min.) will discuss ways to assess machine commonsense abilities, and challenges in developing benchmarks for such evaluations.

Concluding discussion (10 min.) will summarize the remaining challenges of commonsense research, and wrap up the tutorial.

3.2 Breadth

Due to the research interests and output of the presenters, we estimate that approximately 30% of the tutorial will center around work done by the presenters (Rashkin et al., 2018b; Sap et al., 2019a; Bosselut et al., 2019; Rashkin et al., 2018a; Sap et al., 2019b; Zellers et al., 2018, 2019; Sakaguchi et al., 2019; Bosselut and Choi, 2019; Shwartz et al., 2020).

4 Prerequisites

We will not expect attendees to be familiar with previous research on commonsense knowledge representation and reasoning, but participants should be familiar with:

- Knowledge of machine learning and deep learning – recent neural network architectures (e.g., RNN, CNN, Transformers), as well as large pretrained language models models (e.g., BERT, GPT, GPT2).
- Familiarity with natural language processing tasks – understanding the basic problem to solve in tasks such as question answering (QA), natural language generation (NLG), textual entailment/natural language inference (NLI), etc.

5 Reading List

- Storks et al. (2019) – a survey on commonsense
- Levesque (2011) – The Winograd Schema challenge, considered an ideal benchmark for evaluating commonsense reasoning
- Speer et al. (2017) – A description of a prototypical commonsense knowledge base, its structure, and its curation
- Gordon and Van Durme (2013) – Overview of issues surrounding reporting bias, making automatic commonsense acquisition difficult
- Mostafazadeh et al. (2016) – A dataset that appears often in recent commonsense research
- Talmor et al. (2019) – One approach for leveraging crowdsourcing to construct a commonsense evaluation benchmark

6 Instructor information

Maarten Sap is a PhD student in the Paul G. Allen School of Computer Science & Engineering at the University of Washington. His research focuses primarily on social applications of NLP, specifically on endowing machines with social intelligence, social commonsense, or theory of mind.

Vered Shwartz is a postdoctoral researcher at the Allen Institute for Artificial Intelligence (AI2) and the Paul G. Allen School of Computer Science & Engineering at the University of Washington, working on lexical semantics, multiword expressions, and commonsense reasoning. She co-organized the ACL 2018 Student Research Workshop, the SemEval 2018 shared task on hypernymy discovery, and the AAAI 2020 Workshop on Reasoning for Complex Question Answering, Special Edition on Commonsense Reasoning.

Antoine Bosselut is a PhD student in the Paul G. Allen School of Computer Science & Engineering at the University of Washington and a student researcher at the Allen Institute for Artificial Intelligence (AI2). His research interests are in integrating commonsense knowledge and reasoning into downstream applications for text generation, summarization, and conversational dialogue. He organized the West Coast NLP (WeCNLP) in 2018 and 2019 and the NeuralGen workshop at NAACL 2019.

Yejin Choi is an associate professor at the Paul G. Allen School of Computer Science & Engineering at the University of Washington and also a senior research manager at AI2 overseeing the project Mosaic. Her research interests include language grounding with vision, physical and social commonsense knowledge, language generation with long-term coherence, conversational AI, and AI for social good. She was a recipient of Borg Early Career Award (BECA) in 2018, among the IEEEs AI Top 10 to Watch in 2015, a co-recipient of the Marr Prize at ICCV 2013, and a faculty advisor for the Sounding Board team that won the inaugural Alexa Prize Challenge in 2017. She was on the steering committee of the NeuralGen workshop at NAACL 2019.

Dan Roth is the Eduardo D. Glandt Distinguished Professor at the Department of Computer and Information Science, University of Pennsylvania, and a Fellow of the AAAS, the ACM, AAAI, and the ACL. In 2017 Roth was awarded the John McCarthy Award, the highest award the AI community gives to mid-career AI researchers. He was the Editor-in-Chief of the Journal of Artificial Intelligence Research (JAIR) and a program co-chair of AAAI, ACL and CoNLL. Dan has presented several tutorials in conferences including at ACL, on entity linking, temporal reasoning, transferable representation learning, and more.

References

Ian Apperly. 2010. *Mindreaders: the cognitive basis of" theory of mind"*. Psychology Press.

Pratyay Banerjee, Kuntal Kumar Pal, Arindam Mitra, and Chitta Baral. 2019. Careful selection of knowledge to solve open book question answering. In *ACL*.

Simon Baron-Cohen, Alan M Leslie, and Uta Frith. 1985. Does the Autistic Child have a "Theory of Mind"? *Cognition*, 21(1):37–46.

Lisa Bauer, Yicheng Wang, and Mohit Bansal. 2018. Commonsense for generative multi-hop question answering tasks. In *EMNLP*.

Antoine Bosselut and Yejin Choi. 2019. Dynamic Knowledge Graph Construction for Zero-shot Commonsense Question Answering. *ArXiv*, abs/1911.03876.

Antoine Bosselut, Hannah Rashkin, Maarten Sap, Chaitanya Malaviya, Asli Celikyilmaz, and Yejin Choi. 2019. Comet: Commonsense transformers for automatic knowledge graph construction. In *ACL*.

Kenneth Burke. 1969. *A grammar of motives*, volume 177. Univ of California Press.

Nathanael Chambers and Dan Jurafsky. 2008. Unsupervised learning of narrative event chains. In *ACL*, pages 789–797.

Jiaao Chen, Jianshu Chen, and Zhou Yu. 2018. Incorporating structured commonsense knowledge in story completion. In *AAAI*.

Ernest Davis. 2017. Logical formalizations of commonsense reasoning: A survey. *J. Artif. Intell. Res.*, 59:651–723.

Ernest Davis and Gary Marcus. 2015. Commonsense reasoning and commonsense knowledge in artificial intelligence. *Commun. ACM*, 58:92–103.

Jacob Devlin, Ming-Wei Chang, Kenton Lee, and Kristina Toutanova. 2019. Bert: Pre-training of deep bidirectional transformers for language understanding. In *NAACL-HLT*.

Yanai Elazar, Abhijit Mahabal, Deepak Ramachandran, Tania Bedrax-Weiss, and Dan Roth. 2019. How large are lions? inducing distributions over quantitative attributes. In *Proceedings of the 57th Annual Meeting of the Association for Computational Linguistics*, pages 3973–3983, Florence, Italy. Association for Computational Linguistics.

Oren Etzioni, Michele Banko, Stephen Soderland, and Daniel S. Weld. 2008. Open information extraction from the web. In *IJCAI*.

Joshua Feldman, Joe Davison, and Alexander M Rush. 2019. Commonsense knowledge mining from pretrained models. In *EMNLP*.

Kenneth D. Forbus. 1989. Qualitative process theory.

Alvin I Goldman. 2015. *Theory of human action*. Princeton University Press.

Andrew S Gordon and Jerry R Hobbs. 2017. *A Formal Theory of Commonsense Psychology: How People Think People Think*. Cambridge University Press.

Jonathan Gordon and Benjamin Van Durme. 2013. Reporting Bias and Knowledge Extraction. In *Automated Knowledge Base Construction (AKBC) 2013: The 3rd Workshop on Knowledge Extraction, at CIKM*.

Jian Guan, Yansen Wang, and Minlie Huang. 2018. Story ending generation with incremental encoding and commonsense knowledge. In *AAAI*.

David Gunning. 2018. Machine common sense concept paper.

Patrick J. Hayes. 1978. The naive physics manifesto.

Lifu Huang, Ronan Le Bras, Chandra Bhagavatula, and Yejin Choi. 2019. Cosmos qa: Machine reading comprehension with contextual commonsense reasoning. In *EMNLP*, volume abs/1909.00277.

Stanislaw Jastrzebski, Dzmitry Bahdanau, Seyedarian Hosseini, Michael Noukhovitch, Yoshua Bengio, and Jackie Chi Kit Cheung. 2018. Commonsense mining as knowledge base completion? a study on the impact of novelty. In *Workshop on Generalization in the Age of Deep Learning at NAACL*.

Ganesh Jawahar, Benoît Sagot, and Djamé Seddah. 2019. What does BERT learn about the structure of language? In *Proceedings of the 57th Annual Meeting of the Association for Computational Linguistics*, pages 3651–3657, Florence, Italy. Association for Computational Linguistics.

Douglas B. Lenat. 1995. Cyc: A large-scale investment in knowledge infrastructure. *Commun. ACM*, 38:32–38.

Hector J. Levesque. 2011. The winograd schema challenge. In *AAAI Spring Symposium: Logical Formalizations of Commonsense Reasoning*.

Qian Li, Ziwei Li, Jin-Mao Wei, Yanhui Gu, Adam Jatowt, and Zhenglu Yang. 2018. A multi-attention based neural network with external knowledge for story ending predicting task. In *COLING*.

Bill Yuchen Lin, Xinyue Chen, Jamin Chen, and Xiang Ren. 2019. Kagnet: Knowledge-aware graph networks for commonsense reasoning. *ArXiv*, abs/1909.02151.

Hongyu Lin, Le Sun, and Xianpei Han. 2017. Reasoning with heterogeneous knowledge for commonsense machine comprehension. In *Proceedings of the 2017 Conference on Empirical Methods in Natural Language Processing*.

Nelson F Liu, Matt Gardner, Yonatan Belinkov, Matthew Peters, and Noah A Smith. 2019a. Linguistic knowledge and transferability of contextual representations. In *NAACL-HLT*.

Yinhan Liu, Myle Ott, Naman Goyal, Jingfei Du, Mandar S. Joshi, Danqi Chen, Omer Levy, Mike Lewis, Luke S. Zettlemoyer, and Veselin Stoyanov. 2019b. Roberta: A robustly optimized bert pretraining approach.

Peter Lo Bue and Alexander Yates. 2011. Types of Common-Sense knowledge needed for recognizing textual entailment. In *ACL*.

Robert Logan, Nelson F. Liu, Matthew E. Peters, Matt Gardner, and Sameer Singh. 2019. Barack's wife hillary: Using knowledge graphs for fact-aware language modeling. In *Proceedings of the 57th Annual Meeting of the Association for Computational Linguistics*, pages 5962–5971, Florence, Italy. Association for Computational Linguistics.

Gary Marcus. 2018. Deep learning: A critical appraisal.

Ken McRae, George S Cree, Mark S Seidenberg, and Chris McNorgan. 2005. Semantic feature production norms for a large set of living and nonliving things. *Behavior research methods*, 37(4):547–559.

Tzvetan Mihaylov and Anette Frank. 2018. Knowledgeable reader: Enhancing cloze-style reading comprehension with external commonsense knowledge. In *ACL*.

Chris Moore. 2013. *The development of commonsense psychology*. Psychology Press.

Nasrin Mostafazadeh, Nathanael Chambers, Xiaodong He, Mark Johnson, Dhruv Batra, Lucy Vanderwende, Pushmeet Kohli, and James F. Allen. 2016. A corpus and cloze evaluation for deeper understanding of commonsense stories. In *HLT-NAACL*.

Ryan Musa, Xiaoyan Wang, Achille Fokoue, Nicholas Mattei, Maria Chang, Pavan Kapanipathi, Bassem Makni, Kartik Talamadupula, and Michael J. Witbrock. 2019. Answering science exam questions using query reformulation with background knowledge. In *AKBC 2019*.

Simon Ostermann, Michael Roth, Ashutosh Modi, Stefan Thater, and Manfred Pinkal. 2018. SemEval-2018 task 11: Machine comprehension using commonsense knowledge. In *Proceedings of The 12th International Workshop on Semantic Evaluation*.

Debjit Paul and Anette Frank. 2019. Ranking and selecting multi-hop knowledge paths to better predict human needs. *ArXiv*, abs/1904.00676.

Judea Pearl and Dana Mackenzie. 2018. *The book of why: the new science of cause and effect*. Basic Books.

Matthew Peters, Mark Neumann, Mohit Iyyer, Matt Gardner, Christopher Clark, Kenton Lee, and Luke Zettlemoyer. 2018. Deep contextualized word representations. In *NAACL-HLT*, pages 2227–2237.

Fabio Petroni, Tim Rocktäschel, Patrick Lewis, Anton Bakhtin, Yuxiang Wu, Alexander H Miller, and Sebastian Riedel. 2019. Language models as knowledge bases? In *EMNLP*.

Martha E. Pollack. 2005. Intelligent technology for an aging population: The use of ai to assist elders with cognitive impairment. *AI Magazine*, 26:9–24.

Nazneen Fatema Rajani, Bryan McCann, Caiming Xiong, and Richard Socher. 2019. Explain yourself! leveraging language models for commonsense reasoning. In *ACL*.

Hannah Rashkin, Antoine Bosselut, Maarten Sap, Kevin Knight, and Yejin Choi. 2018a. Modeling naive psychology of characters in simple commonsense stories. In *ACL*.

Hannah Rashkin, Maarten Sap, Emily Allaway, Noah A. Smith, and Yejin Choi. 2018b. Event2mind: Commonsense inference on events, intents, and reactions. In *ACL*.

Melissa Roemmele, Cosmin Adrian Bejan, and Andrew S. Gordon. 2011. Semeval-2012 task 7: Choice of plausible alternatives: An evaluation of commonsense causal reasoning. In *SemEval@NAACL-HLT*.

Keisuke Sakaguchi, Ronan Le Bras, Chandra Bhagavatula, and Yejin Choi. 2019. Winogrande: An adversarial winograd schema challenge at scale. *ArXiv*, abs/1907.10641.

Maarten Sap, Ronan LeBras, Emily Allaway, Chandra Bhagavatula, Nicholas Lourie, Hannah Rashkin, Brendan Roof, Noah A Smith, and Yejin Choi. 2019a. Atomic: An atlas of machine commonsense for if-then reasoning. In *AAAI*.

Maarten Sap, Hannah Rashkin, Derek Chen, Ronan LeBras, and Yejin Choi. 2019b. Social iqa: Commonsense reasoning about social interactions. In *EMNLP*.

Roger C. Schank and Robert P. Abelson. 1975. Scripts, plans and knowledge. In *IJCAI*.

Roy Schwartz, Maarten Sap, Ioannis Konstas, Li Zilles, Yejin Choi, and Noah A Smith. 2017. The effect of different writing tasks on linguistic style: A case study of the roc story cloze task. In *CoNLL*.

Vered Shwartz and Ido Dagan. 2019. Still a pain in the neck: Evaluating text representations on lexical composition. *Transactions of the Association for Computational Linguistics*, 7:403–419.

Vered Shwartz, Peter West, Ronan Le Bras, Chandra Bhagavatula, and Yejin Choi. 2020. Unsupervised commonsense question answering with self-talk. In *arXiv cs.CL 2004.05483*.

Robyn Speer, Joshua Chin, and Catherine Havasi. 2017. ConceptNet 5.5: An open multilingual graph of general knowledge. In *AAAI*.

Shane Storks, Qiaozi Gao, and Joyce Yue Chai. 2019. Commonsense reasoning for natural language understanding: A survey of benchmarks, resources, and approaches. *ArXiv*, abs/1904.01172.

Alon Talmor, Jonathan Herzig, Nicholas Lourie, and Jonathan Berant. 2019. Commonsenseqa: A question answering challenge targeting commonsense knowledge. In *NAACL-HLT*.

Niket Tandon, Bhavana Dalvi, Joel Grus, Wen tau Yih, Antoine Bosselut, and Peter Clark. 2018. Reasoning about actions and state changes by injecting commonsense knowledge. In *EMNLP*.

Ian Tenney, Dipanjan Das, and Ellie Pavlick. 2019a. BERT rediscovers the classical NLP pipeline. In *Proceedings of the 57th Annual Meeting of the Association for Computational Linguistics*, pages 4593–4601, Florence, Italy. Association for Computational Linguistics.

Ian Tenney, Patrick Xia, Berlin Chen, Alex Wang, Adam Poliak, R Thomas McCoy, Najoung Kim, Benjamin Van Durme, Sam Bowman, Dipanjan Das, and Ellie Pavlick. 2019b. What do you Learn from Context? Probing for Sentence Structure in Contextualized Word Representations. In *International Conference on Learning Representations*.

Xiaoyan Wang, Pavan Kapanipathi, Ryan Musa, Mo Yu, Kartik Talamadupula, Ibrahim Abdelaziz, Maria Chang, Achille Fokoue, Bassem Makni, Nicholas Mattei, and Michael J. Witbrock. 2018. Improving natural language inference using external knowledge in the science questions domain. In *AAAI*.

Dirk Weissenborn, Tom'avs Kovcisk'y, and Chris Dyer. 2017. Dynamic integration of background knowledge in neural nlu systems. *CoRR*, abs/1706.02596.

Jiangnan Xia, Chenjie Wu, and Ming Yan. 2019. Incorporating relation knowledge into commonsense reading comprehension with multi-task learning. *ArXiv*, abs/1908.04530.

Wenhan Xiong, M. Y. Yu, Shiyu Chang, Xiaoxiao Guo, and William Yang Wang. 2019. Improving question answering over incomplete kbs with knowledge-aware reader. In *ACL*.

Rowan Zellers, Yonatan Bisk, Ali Farhadi, and Yejin Choi. 2018. From recognition to cognition: Visual commonsense reasoning. In *CVPR*.

Rowan Zellers, Ari Holtzman, Yonatan Bisk, Ali Farhadi, and Yejin Choi. 2019. Hellaswag: Can a machine really finish your sentence? In *ACL*.

Shenmin Zhang, Xiaodong Liu, Jingjing Liu, Jianfeng Gao, Kevin Duh, and Benjamin Van Durme. 2018. Record: Bridging the gap between human and machine commonsense reading comprehension. *ArXiv*, abs/1810.12885.

Shenmin Zhang, Rachel Rudinger, Kevin Duh, and Benjamin Van Durme. 2016. Ordinal commonsense inference. *Transactions of the Association for Computational Linguistics*, 5:379–395.

Wanjun Zhong, Duyu Tang, Nan Duan, Ming Zhou, Jiahai Wang, and Jian Yin. 2018. Improving question answering by commonsense-based pre-training. *ArXiv*, abs/1809.03568.

Ben Zhou, Daniel Khashabi, Qiang Ning, and Dan Roth. 2019. "going on a vacation" takes longer than "going for a walk": A study of temporal commonsense understanding. In *EMNLP*, pages 3363–3369, Hong Kong, China. Association for Computational Linguistics.

Hao Zhou, Tom Young, Minlie Huang, Haizhou Zhao, Jingfang Xu, and Xiaoyan Zhu. 2018. Commonsense knowledge aware conversation generation with graph attention. In *IJCAI*.

Open-Domain Question Answering

Danqi Chen
Princeton University
Princeton, NJ
danqic@cs.princeton.edu

Wen-tau Yih
Facebook AI Research
Seattle, WA
scottyih@fb.com

1 Description

Open-domain question answering (QA), the task of answering questions using a large collection of documents of diversified topics, has been a long-standing problem in NLP, information retrieval (IR) and related fields (Voorhees et al., 1999; Moldovan et al., 2000; Brill et al., 2002; Ferrucci et al., 2010). Traditional QA systems were usually constructed as a pipeline, consisting of many different components such as question processing, document/passage retrieval, and answer processing. With the rapid development of neural reading comprehension (Chen, 2018), modern open-domain QA systems have been restructured by combining traditional IR techniques and neural reading comprehension models (Chen et al., 2017; Yang et al., 2019; Min et al., 2019a) or even implemented in a fully end-to-end fashion (Lee et al., 2019; Seo et al., 2019; Guu et al., 2020; Roberts et al., 2020). In this tutorial, we aim to provide a comprehensive and coherent overview of *cutting-edge* research in this direction.[1]

We will start by first giving a brief background of open-domain question answering, discussing the basic setup and core technical challenges of the research problem. We aim to give the audience a historical view of how the field has advanced in the past several decades, from highly-modulated pipeline systems in the early days, to modern end-to-end training of deep neural networks in the present.

We will then discuss modern datasets proposed for open-domain QA (Voorhees et al., 1999; Berant et al., 2013; Rajpurkar et al., 2016; Joshi et al., 2017; Dhingra et al., 2017; Dunn et al., 2017; Kwiatkowski et al., 2019), as well as common evaluation metrics and benchmarks. We plan to provide a detailed discussion on available datasets — their collection methodology and properties — as well as insights on how these datasets should be viewed in the context of open-domain QA.

Next, the focus will shift to cutting-edge models proposed for open-domain QA, which is also the central part of this tutorial. We divide existing models into three main categories: *Two-stage retriever-reader approaches*, *Dense retriever and end-to-end training*, and *Retriever-free approaches*. We will present the logical elements behind different sorts of models and discuss their pros and cons.

Two-stage retriever-reader approaches. We will start by discussing two-stage retriever-reader frameworks for open-domain QA, pioneered by Chen et al. (2017): a *retriever* component finding documents that (might) contain an answer from a large collection of documents, followed by a *reader* component finding the answer in a given paragraph or a document. In this category, the retriever component is usually implemented by traditional sparse vector space methods, such as TF-IDF or BM25 and the reader is implemented by neural reading comprehension models. We will further discuss several challenges and techniques arising in this area, including multi-passage training (Clark and Gardner, 2018; Wang et al., 2019), passage reranking (Wang et al., 2018; Nogueira and Cho, 2019), and denoising distantly-supervised data (Lin et al., 2018).

Dense retriever and end-to-end training. The first category mainly employs a non-machine learning model for the retrieval stage. The second category will focus on how to *learn* the retriever component by replacing traditional IR methods with dense representations, as well as joint training of both components. Learning and searching in dense vector space is challenging, as it usually involves

[1] All the tutorial materials will be released at https://github.com/danqi/acl2020-openqa-tutorial.

Proceedings of the 58th Annual Meeting of the Association for Computational Linguistics, pages 34–37
July 5, 2020.
https://doi.org/10.18653/v1/P17

an enormous search space (easily ranging from millions to billions of documents). We will discuss in depth how this was achieved by existing models, including novel pre-training methods (Lee et al., 2019; Guu et al., 2020), carefully-designed learning algorithms (Karpukhin et al., 2020) or a hybrid approach using both dense and sparse representations (Seo et al., 2019).

Retriever-free approaches. The third category, which is a recent emerging trend, only relies on large-scale pre-trained models (Radford et al., 2018; Devlin et al., 2018; Liu et al., 2019) as implicit knowledge bases and doesn't require access to text data during inference time. These pre-trained models will be used directly to answer questions, in a zero-shot manner (Radford et al., 2019; Raffel et al., 2019) or fine-tuned using question-answer pairs. As these methods don't need a retriever component, we call them *Retriever-free approaches*.

Up to this point, our tutorial has mainly focused on textual question answering. At the end, we also plan to discuss some hybrid approaches for answering open-domain questions using both text and large knowledge bases, such as Freebase (Bollacker et al., 2008) and Wikidata (Vrandečić and Krötzsch, 2014), and give a critical review on how structured data complements the information from unstructured text. The approaches include (1) how to leverage structured data to guide the retriever or reader stage of existing textual QA systems (Asai et al., 2020; Min et al., 2019b), or (2) how to synthesize information from these two heterogeneous sources and build effective QA models on the combined information (Sun et al., 2018, 2019; Xiong et al., 2019).

Finally, we will discuss some important questions, including (1) How much progress have we made compared to the QA systems developed in the last decade? (2) What are the main challenges and limitations of current approaches? (3) How to trade off the efficiency (computational time and memory requirements) and accuracy in the deep learning era? We hope our tutorial will not only serve as a useful resource for the audience to efficiently acquire up-to-date knowledge, but also provide new perspectives to stimulate the advances of open-domain QA research in the next phase.

Prerequisites The tutorial will be accessible to anyone who has the basic knowledge of machine learning and natural language processing. The tutorial will target both NLP researchers/students in academia and NLP practitioners in industry.

2 Tutorial Outline

The intended duration of this tutorial is 3.5 hours, including a half an hour break.

1. Introduction
2. Problem definition & motivation
3. A history of open-domain (textual) QA
   (a) Early QA systems
   (b) TREC QA competitions
   (c) IBM's DeepQA project
   (d) More recent developments: 2017-2020
4. Datasets & evaluation
   (a) Reading comprehension vs QA datasets
   (b) Categorization of QA datasets
   (c) Evaluation metrics
5. Two-stage retriever-reader approaches
   (a) General framework
   (b) Multi-passage training
   (c) Passage reranking
   (d) Denoising distantly supervised data
6. Dense retriever and end-to-end training
   (a) Dense passage retrieval
   (b) Joint training of retriever and reader
   (c) Dense-sparse phrase indexing
7. Retriever-free approaches
8. Open-domain QA using KBs and text
   (a) Improving retriever and reader using structured KBs
   (b) Answering questions over combined KBs and text
9. Open problems and future directions

3 Presenters

Danqi Chen Danqi Chen is an Assistant Professor of Computer Science at Princeton University and co-directs the Princeton NLP Group. Danqi's research interests lie within deep learning for natural language processing, with an emphasis on the intersection between text understanding and knowledge representation/reasoning and applications such as question answering and information extraction. Before joining Princeton University, Danqi worked as a visiting scientist at Facebook AI Research (FAIR). She received her PhD from Stanford University (advised by Christopher Manning) in 2018 and B.Eng from Tsinghua University in 2012. Website: https://www.cs.princeton.edu/~danqic/.

Scott Wen-tau Yih Scott Wen-tau Yih is a Research Scientist at Facebook AI Research (FAIR), and his recent research focuses on continuous representations and neural network models, with applications in knowledge base embedding, semantic parsing and question answering. Yih received the best paper award from CoNLL'11, an outstanding paper award from ACL'15 and has served as an area co-chair and a program co-chair for several top conferences. He is also a co-presenter for several popular tutorials on topics including Semantic Role Labeling, Deep Learning for NLP, Question Answering with Knowledge Base, Web and Beyond and NLP for Precision Medicine. Website: http://scottyih.org/.

References

Akari Asai, Kazuma Hashimoto, Hannaneh Hajishirzi, Richard Socher, and Caiming Xiong. 2020. Learning to retrieve reasoning paths over wikipedia graph for question answering. In *International Conference on Learning Representations (ICLR)*.

Jonathan Berant, Andrew Chou, Roy Frostig, and Percy Liang. 2013. Semantic parsing on Freebase from question-answer pairs. In *Empirical Methods in Natural Language Processing (EMNLP)*, pages 1533–1544.

Kurt Bollacker, Colin Evans, Praveen Paritosh, Tim Sturge, and Jamie Taylor. 2008. Freebase: a collaboratively created graph database for structuring human knowledge. In *ACM SIGMOD international conference on Management of data*, pages 1247–1250.

Eric Brill, Susan Dumais, and Michele Banko. 2002. An analysis of the AskMSR question-answering system. In *Empirical Methods in Natural Language Processing (EMNLP)*, pages 257–264.

Danqi Chen. 2018. *Neural Reading Comprehension and Beyond*. Ph.D. thesis, Stanford University.

Danqi Chen, Adam Fisch, Jason Weston, and Antoine Bordes. 2017. Reading Wikipedia to answer open-domain questions. In *Association for Computational Linguistics (ACL)*, pages 1870–1879.

Christopher Clark and Matt Gardner. 2018. Simple and effective multi-paragraph reading comprehension. In *Association for Computational Linguistics (ACL)*, pages 845–855.

Jacob Devlin, Ming-Wei Chang, Kenton Lee, and Kristina Toutanova. 2018. BERT: Pre-training of deep bidirectional transformers for language understanding. *arXiv preprint arXiv:1810.04805*.

Bhuwan Dhingra, Kathryn Mazaitis, and William W Cohen. 2017. Quasar: Datasets for question answering by search and reading. *arXiv preprint arXiv:1707.03904*.

Matthew Dunn, Levent Sagun, Mike Higgins, V Ugur Guney, Volkan Cirik, and Kyunghyun Cho. 2017. SearchQA: A new Q&A dataset augmented with context from a search engine. *arXiv preprint arXiv:1704.05179*.

David Ferrucci, Eric Brown, Jennifer Chu-Carroll, James Fan, David Gondek, Aditya A Kalyanpur, Adam Lally, J William Murdock, Eric Nyberg, John Prager, et al. 2010. Building Watson: An overview of the DeepQA project. *AI magazine*, 31(3):59–79.

Kelvin Guu, Kenton Lee, Zora Tung, Panupong Pasupat, and Ming-Wei Chang. 2020. REALM: Retrieval-augmented language model pre-training. *arXiv preprint arXiv:2002.08909*.

Mandar Joshi, Eunsol Choi, Daniel S Weld, and Luke Zettlemoyer. 2017. TriviaQA: A large scale distantly supervised challenge dataset for reading comprehension. In *Association for Computational Linguistics (ACL)*, pages 1601–1611.

Vladimir Karpukhin, Barlas Oğuz, Sewon Min, Ledell Wu, Sergey Edunov, Danqi Chen, and Wen-tau Yih. 2020. Dense passage retrieval for open-domain question answering. *arXiv preprint arXiv:2004.04906*.

Tom Kwiatkowski, Jennimaria Palomaki, Olivia Redfield, Michael Collins, Ankur Parikh, Chris Alberti, Danielle Epstein, Illia Polosukhin, Jacob Devlin, Kenton Lee, Kristina Toutanova, Llion Jones, Matthew Kelcey, Ming-Wei Change, Andrew M. Dai, Jakob Uszkoreit, Quoc Le, and Slav Petrov. 2019. Natural questions: a benchmark for question answering research. *Transactions of the Association of Computational Linguistics (TACL)*.

Kenton Lee, Ming-Wei Chang, and Kristina Toutanova. 2019. Latent retrieval for weakly supervised open domain question answering. In *Association for Computational Linguistics (ACL)*, pages 6086–6096.

Yankai Lin, Haozhe Ji, Zhiyuan Liu, and Maosong Sun. 2018. Denoising distantly supervised open-domain question answering. In *Association for Computational Linguistics (ACL)*, pages 1736–1745.

Yinhan Liu, Myle Ott, Naman Goyal, Jingfei Du, Mandar Joshi, Danqi Chen, Omer Levy, Mike Lewis, Luke Zettlemoyer, and Veselin Stoyanov. 2019. RoBERTa: A robustly optimized BERT pretraining approach. *arXiv preprint arXiv:1907.11692*.

Sewon Min, Danqi Chen, Hannaneh Hajishirzi, and Luke Zettlemoyer. 2019a. A discrete hard EM approach for weakly supervised question answering. In *Empirical Methods in Natural Language Processing (EMNLP)*.

Sewon Min, Danqi Chen, Luke Zettlemoyer, and Hannaneh Hajishirzi. 2019b. Knowledge guided text retrieval and reading for open domain question answering. *arXiv preprint arXiv:1911.03868*.

Dan Moldovan, Sanda Harabagiu, Marius Pasca, Rada Mihalcea, Roxana Girju, Richard Goodrum, and Vasile Rus. 2000. The structure and performance of an open-domain question answering system. In *Association for Computational Linguistics (ACL)*, pages 563–570.

Rodrigo Nogueira and Kyunghyun Cho. 2019. Passage re-ranking with BERT. *arXiv preprint arXiv:1901.04085*.

Alec Radford, Karthik Narasimhan, Tim Salimans, and Ilya Sutskever. 2018. Improving language understanding by generative pre-training. Technical report, OpenAI.

Alec Radford, Jeffrey Wu, Rewon Child, David Luan, Dario Amodei, and Ilya Sutskever. 2019. Language models are unsupervised multitask learners. Technical report, OpenAI.

Colin Raffel, Noam Shazeer, Adam Roberts, Katherine Lee, Sharan Narang, Michael Matena, Yanqi Zhou, Wei Li, and Peter J Liu. 2019. Exploring the limits of transfer learning with a unified text-to-text transformer. *arXiv preprint arXiv:1910.10683*.

Pranav Rajpurkar, Jian Zhang, Konstantin Lopyrev, and Percy Liang. 2016. SQuAD: 100,000+ questions for machine comprehension of text. In *Empirical Methods in Natural Language Processing (EMNLP)*, pages 2383–2392.

Adam Roberts, Colin Raffel, and Noam Shazeer. 2020. How much knowledge can you pack into the parameters of a language model? *arXiv preprint arXiv:2002.08910*.

Minjoon Seo, Jinhyuk Lee, Tom Kwiatkowski, Ankur Parikh, Ali Farhadi, and Hannaneh Hajishirzi. 2019. Real-time open-domain question answering with dense-sparse phrase index. In *Association for Computational Linguistics (ACL)*, pages 4430–4441.

Haitian Sun, Tania Bedrax-Weiss, and William W Cohen. 2019. PullNet: Open domain question answering with iterative retrieval on knowledge bases and text. In *Empirical Methods in Natural Language Processing (EMNLP)*.

Haitian Sun, Bhuwan Dhingra, Manzil Zaheer, Kathryn Mazaitis, Ruslan Salakhutdinov, and William Cohen. 2018. Open domain question answering using early fusion of knowledge bases and text. In *Empirical Methods in Natural Language Processing (EMNLP)*, pages 4231–4242.

Ellen M Voorhees et al. 1999. The TREC-8 question answering track report. In *Trec*, volume 99, pages 77–82. Citeseer.

Denny Vrandečić and Markus Krötzsch. 2014. Wikidata: a free collaborative knowledge base.

Shuohang Wang, Mo Yu, Xiaoxiao Guo, Zhiguo Wang, Tim Klinger, Wei Zhang, Shiyu Chang, Gerald Tesauro, Bowen Zhou, and Jing Jiang. 2018. R^3: Reinforced reader-ranker for open-domain question answering. In *Conference on Artificial Intelligence (AAAI)*.

Zhiguo Wang, Patrick Ng, Xiaofei Ma, Ramesh Nallapati, and Bing Xiang. 2019. Multi-passage bert: A globally normalized bert model for open-domain question answering. In *Empirical Methods in Natural Language Processing (EMNLP)*, pages 5881–5885.

Wenhan Xiong, Mo Yu, Shiyu Chang, Xiaoxiao Guo, and William Yang Wang. 2019. Improving question answering over incomplete kbs with knowledge-aware reader. In *Association for Computational Linguistics (ACL)*, pages 4258–4264.

Wei Yang, Yuqing Xie, Aileen Lin, Xingyu Li, Luchen Tan, Kun Xiong, Ming Li, and Jimmy Lin. 2019. End-to-end open-domain question answering with bertserini. In *North American Association for Computational Linguistics (NAACL)*, pages 72–77.

Author Index

Association for Computational Linguistics
209 N. Eighth Street
Stroudsburg, Pennsylvania 18360

ISBN 978-1-7138-1374-3

CURRAN ASSOCIATES INC.
proceedings.com